NUMBER AND ALGEBRA

NUMBER AND ALGEBRA

GOLF GAME

a) Lion Forest, the world's best golfer, played 9 holes of golf. He finished the course in 33 strokes.

He scored the same number of 3s and 4s and he completed one hole in 5 strokes.

How many holes did Lion complete in 4 strokes?

b) In his next round of 18 holes, Lion Forest finished the course in 70 strokes.

He completed 6 of the holes in 3 strokes.

He completed the remaining holes in either 4 or 5 strokes.

How many holes did Lion complete in 4 strokes and 5 strokes?

Extension

Shan played 18 holes of golf. He scored twice as many 5s as he scored 4s, and twice as many 4s as he scored 3s. He completed the other 4 holes in 6 shots.

What was Shan's score for the 18 holes?

Strategy hints!

1. Look for the important words in the question.
4. Use a table or a chart.
9. Think logically.

ISBN 978 1 4202 9396 8

NUMBERS

a) Two numbers add up to 19 and differ by 5.
What is the product of the 2 numbers?

b) Two numbers add up to 18 and have a product of 65.
What are the 2 numbers?

Extension

3 numbers multiply together to equal 280.
They differ by 3 and then by 3 again.
What are the 3 numbers?

Strategy hints!

1 Look for the important words in the question.

9 Think logically.

ISBN 978 1 4202 9396 8

STARTING NUMBER

a) A number is doubled. Then 4 is added to it. Then it is multiplied by 10. The answer is 80.

What was the starting number?

b) A number is doubled, then doubled, then tripled. The answer is 84.

What was the starting number?

Extension

Jane is given a bag of marbles. She gives half of the marbles to Ava and a quarter of what is left to Rosie. Rosie now has 8 marbles.

How many marbles were originally in the bag?

Strategy hints!

1 Look for the important words in the question.

3 Have a go.

6 Work backwards.

ISBN 978 1 4202 9396 8

LIGHT BAR LOGIC

27 uses 9 light bars when shown on a calculator.

a) What are the 2 smallest 2-digit numbers that use 9 light bars when shown on a calculator?

b) What are the 2 biggest 2-digit numbers that use 9 light bars when shown on a calculator?

Extension

a) What are the 2 smallest 3-digit numbers that use 9 light bars when shown on a calculator?

b) What are the 2 biggest 3-digit numbers that use 9 light bars when shown on a calculator?

Strategy hints!

1. Look for the important words in the question.
2. Look for a pattern.
9. Think logically.

ISBN 978 1 4202 9396 8

DECIMAL DELIGHT

a) Use the digits 2, 4 and 7 to make a number that is bigger than 3, but smaller than 4.5.

b) Use the digits 5, 0, 6 and 7 to make a number that is bigger than 6, but smaller than 6.5.

Extension

Use some or all of the digits 1, 3, 8, 5 and 7 to make 5 numbers that are bigger than 13, but smaller than 13.7.

Strategy hints!

1 Look for the important words in the question.

3 Have a go.

9 Think logically.

ISBN 978 1 4202 9396 8

MAKE THAT SUM

a) Use the numbers 1, 2, 3 and 4 in that order, along with +, −, x or ÷ signs to create a sum that equals 32.

b) Use the numbers 1, 2, 3 and 4 in that order, along with +, −, x or ÷ signs to create a sum that equals 36.

Extension

a) Use the numbers 1, 2, 3 and 4 in that order, along with +, −, x or ÷ signs to create 2 different sums that each equal 0.

b) Use the numbers 1, 2, 3 and 4 in that order, along with +, −, x or ÷ signs to create 2 different sums that each equal 1.

Strategy hints!

1 Look for the important words in the question.

3 Have a go.

9 Think logically.

ISBN 978 1 4202 9396 8

CINEMA SEATS

In a cinema, the seat tickets are sold from front row to back row. There are 26 seats in each row and 26 rows in the cinema. The front row seats are named AA, then AB, then AC and so on.

a) Ezra buys ticket BC.
How many tickets were sold before Ezra bought his ticket?

b) How many tickets were sold when ticket FC was handed out?

Extension

a) What was the 351st seat to be sold?

b) What was the 545th seat to be sold?

Strategy hints!

1. Look for the important words in the question.
2. Look for a pattern.

ISBN 978 1 4202 9396 8

CARS AND TRUCKS

The Traffic Authority is doing a survey at a busy street in a light industrial area. For every 9 cars that passed a certain survey point, 4 trucks went by.

a) 78 vehicles pass the survey point. How many are cars and how many are trucks?

b) 100 trucks pass the survey point. How many cars pass during this time?

Extension

The Traffic Authority is doing a second survey at a busy street in a heavy industrial area. The number of trucks to cars that passed the survey point was double compared to the number in the first survey.

How many trucks had passed the survey point when the vehicle count reached 340?

Strategy hints!

1 Look for the important words in the question.

2 Look for a pattern.

4 Use a table or a chart.

ISBN 978 1 4202 9396 8

WHAT NUMBER AM I?

I am a 5-digit number. All my digits are different.
My 10 000s digit and my 1s digit add up to 12.
My 10 000s digit is the biggest digit in my number.
My 1s digit is the 3rd odd number.
My 100s digit is shown by 2 light bars on a calculator.
My 10s digit equals 2 multiplied by itself.
I am bigger than 75 000.

What number am I?

Extension

Make up more problems like this one. See if a classmate can work them out.

Strategy hints!

1 Look for the important words in the question.

9 Think logically.

ISBN 978 1 4202 9396 8

EQUAL NOTES

Bree has an equal number of every note in her purse.
She counts her money and sees that the total is $370.

How many of each note does Bree have in her purse?

Extension

Rachael has $300 in her purse.
She has an equal number of 3 different types of notes.
What are the notes in Rachael's purse?

Strategy hints!

1 Look for the important words in the question.

3 Have a go.

4 Use a table or a chart.

ISBN 978 1 4202 9396 8

MULTIPLICATION MYSTERY

a) What number, when multiplied by itself, equals half of 98?

b) What number, when multiplied by itself, equals 3 lots of 48?

Extension

a) What number, when multiplied by itself, equals 2 x 2 x 2 x 2 x 2 x 2?

b) What number, when multiplied by itself, equals the 61st odd number?

Strategy hints!

1 Look for the important words in the question.

3 Have a go.

9 Think logically.

ISBN 978 1 4202 9396 8

THIRD BIGGEST

a) What is the 3rd biggest 5-digit number that can be made by using 3, 4, 6, 8 and 2?

b) What is the 3rd biggest 5-digit number that can be made by using 4, 5, 4, 3 and 5?

Extension

What is the 3rd biggest 5-digit number that uses 4 different odd numbers and an even number that has been multiplied by itself?

Strategy hints!

1. Look for the important words in the question.
2. Look for a pattern.
9. Think logically.

ISBN 978 1 4202 9396 8

POSTAGE PAID

Every time you post something with Air Acme Delivery, you pay a $5 fee.
On top of that, the company charges 60 cents for every letter or small package it collects.
This morning, Air Acme Delivery collected a total of 25 letters and small packages from our dispatch office.

How much did this cost?

Extension

On a different day, we sent a large number of items with Air Acme Delivery. The delivery costs were the same as above.
Our bill came to $42.20.
What is the total number of letters and small packages that we sent with Air Acme Delivery that day?

Strategy hints!

1 Look for the important words in the question.
4 Use a table or a chart.

ISBN 978 1 4202 9396 8

SEEMS TOO HARD

Find a quick way to solve these problems:

a) 26 x 25 – 24 x 25 = ?

b) 32 x 12 – 31 x 12 = ?

Extension

Find a quick way to solve these problems:

a) 888 x 17 + 112 x 17 = ?

b) 37 x 126 + 43 x 126 + 20 x 126 = ?

Strategy hints!

1. Look for the important words in the question.
7. Try an easier problem.

ISBN 978 1 4202 9396 8

DECIMAL HUNT

I am a 2-digit number with a 1-digit decimal. I am bigger than 54 but smaller than 56. 2 of my digits are even.
When you divide my whole number by the digit in my decimal place, the answer has no remainder.
What are the biggest and smallest numbers I could be?

Extension

I am a 2-digit number with a 2-digit decimal. I am bigger than 20, but smaller than 40. 2 of my digits are even and 2 of my digits are odd. None of my digits are zeroes.
When you divide my whole number by the 2-digit number in my decimal place, the answer has no remainder and is bigger than 1.
What are the biggest and smallest numbers I could be?

Strategy hints!

1 Look for the important words in the question.
9 Think logically.

ISBN 978 1 4202 9396 8

RADIO WAVES

My favourite FM radio station is 101.8.

a) My mum listens to a radio station that is the same distance from 100.0 as my radio station, but is below 100.
What radio station does Mum listen to?

b) My dad listens to a radio station that is halfway between my mum's radio station and 100.0.
What radio station does Dad listen to?

Extension

My sister has a favourite radio station. When rounded to the nearest whole number it equals 105.
It has more odd digits than even digits. One of the digits is zero. It would be shown by 16 light bars on a calculator.
It has 1 decimal place.
What radio station does my sister listen to?

Strategy hints!

1 Look for the important words in the question.

5 Use a drawing.

ISBN 978 1 4202 9396 8

BIGGEST PRODUCT

a) What is the biggest product that can be found by using 1, 2, 3 and 4 to make a sum in which a 3-digit number is multiplied by a 1-digit number?

b) What is the biggest product that can be found by using 1, 2, 3 and 4 to make a sum in which a 2-digit number is multiplied by a 2-digit number?

Extension

a) What are the 2 biggest products that can be found by using 5, 2, 3, 7 and 4 to make sums in which a 4-digit number is multiplied by a 1-digit number?

b) What are the 2 biggest products that can be found by using 5, 2, 3, 7 and 4 to make sums in which a 3-digit number is multiplied by a 2-digit number?

Strategy hints!

1. Look for the important words in the question.
3. Have a go.
9. Think logically.

ISBN 978 1 4202 9396 8

COIN COUNT

Katrina puts all of her coins onto a table. She then groups them.
Katrina puts them into groups of 2, then into groups of 5, then into groups of 6.
Each time, there is one coin left over.

a) What is the smallest number of coins that Katrina could have?

b) What is the smallest amount of money that Katrina could have?

Extension

Craig puts all of his coins onto a table. He then groups them.
Craig puts them into groups of 2, then into groups of 5, then into groups of 7. Each time, there is one coin left over.

a) What is the smallest number of coins that Craig could have?

b) What is the smallest amount of money that Craig could have?

Strategy hints!

1 Look for the important words in the question.

3 Have a go.

9 Think logically.

ISBN 978 1 4202 9396 8

CONSECUTIVE NUMBERS

Numbers that are next to each other, like 4 and 5, are called consecutive numbers.

a) 3 consecutive numbers add up to 39.
What are the 3 numbers?

b) 3 consecutive even numbers add up to 72.
What is the smallest of the numbers?

Extension

3 consecutive numbers that are in the 4 times table add up to 156.
What is the biggest of the numbers?

Strategy hints!

1 Look for the important words in the question.

3 Have a go.

7 Try an easier problem.

ISBN 978 1 4202 9396 8

Focus Number and place value

- Addition
- Subtraction

UP AND DOWN

Scott and Serena play a counting game.

Scott starts at 3 and skip counts upwards by 4s, like this: 3, 7, 11, 15 . . .

At the same time, Serena starts at 100 and skip counts downwards by 4s, like this: 100, 96, 92, 88 . . .

After 1 turn, Scott is on 7 and Serena is on 96.

What is the closest point that Scott and Serena will reach in this game?

Extension

James starts at 0 and skip counts upwards by halves, like this: 0, 0.5, 1, 1.5, 2 . . .

At the same time, Diane starts at 100 and skip counts downwards by 3s, like this: 100, 97, 94, 91 . . .

After 1 turn, James is on 0.5 and Diane is on 97.

What is the closest point that James and Diane will reach in this game?

Strategy hints!

1. Look for the important words in the question.
2. Look for a pattern.
3. Have a go.

ISBN 978 1 4202 9396 8

QUADLEY NUMBERS

A quadley number is a number whose digits are all different.
The digits that are next to each other differ by 4.
Quadley numbers do not have a 4 in them.
There are eight 2-digit quadley numbers.

Find these 8 numbers.

Extension

There are only 2 other quadley numbers. They are both 3-digit numbers.

Find these 2 numbers.

Strategy hints!

1. Look for the important words in the question.
2. Look for a pattern.
9. Think logically.

ISBN 978 1 4202 9396 8

LETTERS AND NUMBERS

a) Y + Z = 11

Y x Z = 24

Y is less than Z.

What numbers are Y and Z?

b) P and Q are both even, 1-digit numbers.

P is bigger than Q.

P x Q is 20 more than P + Q.

What numbers are P and Q?

Extension

D, E and F are 3 different numbers. They are all less than 10.

Together, they add up to 20.

Together, they multiply to 252.

What is the difference between the biggest and the smallest of the 3 numbers?

Strategy hints!

1 Look for the important words in the question.

9 Think logically.

ISBN 978 1 4202 9396 8

PHONE NUMBERS

a) The digits of my 9-digit phone number add up to 49.
The first 3 digits are 2, 9 and 9.
The 8th and 9th digits are 2 and 6.
My phone number is the biggest number that follows these rules.
What is my phone number?

b) The digits of my friend Matilda's 9-digit telephone number add up to 36.
The first 3 digits are 2, 9 and 9.
Her phone number is the 3rd smallest number that follows these rules.
What is Matilda's phone number?

Extension

a) Find the 2 biggest 9-digit phone numbers that start with 2, 9 and 9 and have digits that add up to 22.

b) Find the 2 smallest 9-digit phone numbers that start with 2, 9 and 9 and have digits that add up to 22.

Strategy hints!

1. Look for the important words in the question.
3. Have a go.
9. Think logically.

ISBN 978 1 4202 9396 8

NUMBER CODE

A stands for a digit from 0 to 9.
B stands for a different digit from 0 to 9.
AB + AB + A = 56

a) What does AB stand for?

b) Find the answer to this problem:

BA − AB = ?

Extension

K stands for a 1-digit number.
L stands for a different 1-digit number.
K x K + L x L = 85
What do K and L stand for?

Strategy hints!

1 Look for the important words in the question.

3 Have a go.

9 Think logically.

ISBN 978 1 4202 9396 8

NOTES

a) Dean has 5 notes in his wallet.
He has 4 different types of notes.
Dean has the 2nd smallest amount of money that he can have with this combination.
How much money is in Dean's wallet?

b) Jared has 6 notes in his wallet.
He has $175 in total.
3 of the notes are the same as each other. 3 of the notes are all different to each other.
What notes are in Jared's wallet?

Extension

Phoebe has 12 notes in her wallet. She has $400 in total.
She has 2 examples of 3 types of notes and 3 examples of 2 types of notes.

How many $20 notes does Phoebe have?

Strategy hints!

1. Look for the important words in the question.
3. Have a go.
4. Use a table or a chart.

ISBN 978 1 4202 9396 8

COMPUTER RULES

A computer is programmed to change numbers that are entered in according to a rule.
Here are numbers that have been entered into the computer:

IN 6 OUT 31 IN 4 OUT 11 IN 8 OUT 59

a) Frances enters 12 into the computer. What number will come out?
b) Frances enters 15 into the computer. What number will come out?

Extension

A different computer is programmed to change numbers that are entered in according to a rule.
Here are numbers that have been entered into the computer:

IN 8 OUT 8
IN 12 OUT 10
IN 30 OUT 19

What is this computer programmed to do?

Strategy hints!

1 Look for the important words in the question.
2 Look for a pattern.
4 Use a table or a chart.

ISBN 978 1 4202 9396 8

COMPUTER CRUNCHER

A computer is programmed to change numbers that are entered in according to a rule.
Here are numbers that have been entered into the computer:

IN 8 OUT 4.8 IN 12 OUT 6.12 IN 30 OUT 15.3

What is this computer programmed to do?

Extension

A different computer is programmed to change numbers that are entered in according to a rule.
Here are numbers that have been entered into the computer:

IN 6 OUT 9 IN 4 OUT 5

IN 8 OUT 13 IN 1.5 OUT 0

Heather enters 12 into the computer.
What number will come out?

Strategy hints!

1 Look for the important words in the question.

2 Look for a pattern.

4 Use a table or a chart.

ISBN 978 1 4202 9396 8

PALINDROMIC PALS

Palindromic numbers are the same forwards and backwards, like 22, 131 and 2332.

a) How many palindromic numbers are there between 1000 and 3000?

b) Find the 2nd biggest 6-digit palindromic number that looks like this:

8 □ 4 □ □ □

Extension

You can turn most numbers into a palindromic number by adding its digits backwards. Sometimes you need to do this more than once.

For example: The palindrome of 36: 36 + 63 = 99

The palindrome of 49: 49 + 94 = 143 and 143 + 341 = 484

a) Use this method to turn 3462 into a palindromic number.

b) Make up more problems like this one. See if a classmate can work them out.

Strategy hints!

1 Look for the important words in the question.

2 Look for a pattern.

9 Think logically.

ISBN 978 1 4202 9396 8

SNAKES AND LADDERS

Marco is playing Snakes and Ladders with two 6-sided dice.

He is on 41.

His last 5 moves have been:

+ 8, + 11, − 15 (snake), + 4, − 6 (snake)

What number was Marco on 5 moves ago?

Extension

A player in a Snakes and Ladders game moves forward 10, then slides back 3, then moves forward 10, then slides back 3, and so on.

How many moves will it take to get from 41 to 100?

Strategy hints!

1 Look for the important words in the question.

6 Work backwards.

9 Think logically.

ISBN 978 1 4202 9396 8

SPILT MILK

Kristine wrote down a 4-digit password.
She then spilt her cup of milk, which blurred the last 2 digits of the password.
This is what was left of the password:

8 6 __ __

Kristine remembered that the 4-digit password was in the 3 times table and the 5 times table.

What is the smallest number that the 4-digit password could be?

Extension

A 4-digit password starts with 8 and ends in 4.
It is in the 4 times table.
What is the biggest number that the password could be?

Strategy hints!

1. Look for the important words in the question.
2. Look for a pattern.
9. Think logically.

ISBN 978 1 4202 9396 8

SHORT CUT

Find a quick way to solve these problems:

a) $81 \times 6 - 79 \times 6 = ?$

b) $178 \times 6 - 173 \times 6 = ?$

Extension

Find a quick way to solve these problems:

a) $66 \times 7 + 35 \times 7 = ?$

b) $1400 \div 28 \times 2 = ?$

Strategy hints!

1. Look for the important words in the question.
2. Look for a pattern.
7. Try an easier problem.

ISBN 978 1 4202 9396 8

PIZZA PARTY

For my birthday I invited some friends to my house. We had pizza and watched a movie.

We bought 4 pizzas. My dad cut each pizza up into 8 equal pieces.

Before my friends arrived, Dad ate $\frac{1}{2}$ of one of the pizzas.

How many slices were left for my friends?

Extension

If $3\frac{1}{2}$ pizzas were shared equally among 4 people, how much would each person eat?

Strategy hints!

1 Look for the important words in the question.

5 Use a drawing.

ISBN 978 1 4202 9396 8

CALCULATOR CHALLENGE

Richard wanted to type [25] [x] [5] [x] [2] into his calculator, but he made a mistake. The answer on his screen was 25 times smaller than it should have been.

What had Richard typed into his calculator?

Extension

If you type [3] [x] [=] [=] into a calculator, the answer on the screen will be 27.

Without using a calculator, figure out what the answer on the screen will be if you type:

a) [4] [x] [=] [=]

b) [5] [x] [=] [=]

Strategy hints!

1 Look for the important words in the question.

9 Think logically.

ISBN 978 1 4202 9396 8

CHRISTMAS LIGHTS

On a Christmas tree, lights have been strung up in a special pattern.
Every 6th light is red. Every 7th light is green. Every 8th light is blue. Every other light is yellow.

a) What is the first place where there will be 2 different coloured lights in the same place?

b) How many places in the first 100 will have 2 different coloured lights in the same place?

Extension

There are 4 lighthouses on the coast near a busy shipping lane.

One lighthouse flashes every 4 seconds, one flashes every 5 seconds, one flashes every 6 seconds and one flashes every 8 seconds.

All the lights flash at the same time. How long will it be before they all flash together again?

Strategy hints!

1. Look for the important words in the question.
2. Look for a pattern.
4. Use a table or a chart.

ISBN 978 1 4202 9396 8

JAMES FROND

a) Secret Agent James Frond is sending a message in a secret code.
He uses numbers to stand for letters.
The letters have been moved around slightly from their usual order in the alphabet.
His message is:

15 11 4 26 18 4   7 4 11 15!

What is James' message?

b) James receives a reply in a slightly different code. The reply is:

16 15   21 9 6   24 2 26

What is the reply?

Extension

Create your own secret code and send a message to a classmate. See if they can work it out.

Strategy hints!

1. Look for the important words in the question.
2. Look for a pattern.
9. Think logically.

ISBN 978 1 4202 9396 8

BOOKWORM

Zelda reads whenever she gets a chance.
On the way to school this morning, she read 3 pages of a novel.
The pages she read added up to 45.
After she read these 3 pages, she was halfway through the novel.

How many pages are in Zelda's novel?

Extension

a) The first 2 pages of a book and its last 2 pages add up to 106. How many pages are in the book?

b) The first 2 pages of a book and its last 2 pages add up to 194. How many pages are in the book?

Strategy hints!

1 Look for the important words in the question.

3 Have a go.

9 Think logically.

ISBN 978 1 4202 9396 8

SHOE SIZES

a) My shoe size added to my sister's shoe size equals 7.
My shoe size is 2 sizes bigger than my sister's.
What shoe sizes do we take?

b) My shoe size added to my mum's shoe size and my dad's shoe size equals 21.
Our 3 sizes form a pattern. The difference between my size and Mum's size and then between Mum's size and Dad's size is equal.
Using my shoe size from part **a)**, what shoe sizes do my mum and dad take?

Extension

4 shoes are in a line.
They are all different lengths.
The difference between the 4 shoes doubles from shoe to shoe.
The total of the 4 shoe sizes is $15\frac{1}{2}$.
What size is the shortest shoe?

Strategy hints!

1. Look for the important words in the question.
3. Have a go.
5. Use a drawing.

ISBN 978 1 4202 9396 8

PETALS

A flower contains 50 petals.
On day 1, it drops 1 petal. Each day, it drops 1 more petal than it did the day before.

a) How many petals will be left on the flower at the end of day 6?

b) On which day will the flower drop its last petal?

Extension

On day 1, a flower drops 1 petal. Each day, it drops 1 more petal than it did the day before.

Once all the petals have fallen, its owner sweeps up 153 petals from the ground beneath its pot.

How many days did it take for all the petals to fall?

Strategy hints!

1 Look for the important words in the question.

4 Use a table or a chart.

ISBN 978 1 4202 9396 8

ALL VALUES

What is the smallest amount of notes and coins you need to have to be able to make:

a) All the dollar values from $1 to $20?

b) All the dollar values from $20 to $100?

Extension

Imagine there are only coins valued at 1 cent, 2 cents and 5 cents in our money system.

What is the smallest amount of coins you need to have to be able to make every possible value up to $1?

Strategy hints!

1 Look for the important words in the question.

4 Use a table or a chart.

ISBN 978 1 4202 9396 8

Focus Money and financial mathematics
- Addition

BUYING LETTERS

The Letter Shop is having a sale on its products.
Vowels cost 50 cents each.
Consonants cost 20 cents each.
There is a 10 cent discount on any repeated consonants.
David bought his name for 20 cents + 50 cents + 20 cents + 50 cents + 10 cents.

a) Constantine bought the letters in his name. How much did they cost?

b) Annabelle bought the letters in her name. How much did they cost?

c) Ferdinand bought the letters in his name. How much did they cost?

Extension

If you bought the letters in your first, middle and last name from the Letter Shop, what would it cost?

Strategy hints!

1. Look for the important words in the question.
4. Use a table or a chart.

ISBN 978 1 4202 9396 8

DOGS AND CATS

A cat takes 3 steps to walk the same distance that a dog can walk in 2 steps.

a) A dog and a cat start at the same point and walk 6 steps.
The dog stops to let the cat catch up.
How many steps does the cat need to take to catch up to the dog?

b) A cat walks 54 steps and reaches a puddle.
How many steps will a dog take to reach the same puddle from the same starting point?

Extension

A small dog takes 5 steps to walk the same distance that a large dog can walk in 2 steps.
They take steps at the same time and walk around a 100 m track.

How many metres has the small dog walked when the large dog has completed 2 laps of the track?

Strategy hints!

1. Look for the important words in the question.
4. Use a table or a chart.
9. Think logically.

ISBN 978 1 4202 9396 8

WHO AM I?

I am a 5-digit number.
4 of my digits are even and one of my digits is zero.
All of my digits are different.
I am the 5th biggest number that fits these clues.

What number am I?

Extension

I am a 5-digit number.
All of my digits are odd.
All of my digits are different.
I am the 7th smallest number that fits these clues.

What number am I?

Strategy hints!

1 Look for the important words in the question.

9 Think logically.

ISBN 978 1 4202 9396 8

SKIP COUNT

Jackson and Fiona decide to count upwards from zero.
Jackson skip counts by 7s and Fiona skip counts by 8s.

What are the first 2 numbers that they will both count?

Extension

Hector, David and Tina decide to count upwards from zero.
Hector skip counts by 5s.
David skip counts by 6s.
Tina skip counts by 7s.
Which numbers will all 3 of them count up to 1000?

Strategy hints!

1. Look for the important words in the question.
2. Look for a pattern.
4. Use a table or a chart.

ISBN 978 1 4202 9396 8

PETER IN A LIFT

Peter is in a building.
He gets into a lift and goes down 6 levels.
He is now on a level that is only $\frac{1}{3}$ as high as when he entered the lift.

On which level did Peter enter the lift?

Extension

The following day Peter is in the building again.
He gets into the lift at a level higher than the 1st level.
He then goes up some levels to deliver a package.
Then Peter enters the lift and goes down 2 levels.
He is now on a level that is 4 times as high as when he first entered the lift.

What is the lowest level that Peter could now be on?

Strategy hints!

1 Look for the important words in the question.

5 Use a drawing.

9 Think logically.

ISBN 978 1 4202 9396 8

BUSY POOL

A busy pool has 6 swimming lanes. There are 126 swimmers in the pool. One afternoon, the 1st lane has twice the number of swimmers in it as the 2nd lane. At the same time, the 2nd lane has twice the number of swimmers in it as the 3rd lane, the 3rd lane has twice the number of swimmers in it as the 4th lane, the 4th lane has twice the number of swimmers in it as the 5th lane, and the 5th lane has twice the number of swimmers in it as the 6th lane.

How many swimmers are in the 3rd lane?

Extension

Next morning at 9:00, 21 swimmers are in the pool. Then, 3 more people dive in and some people get out. Now there are only $\frac{2}{3}$ the amount of people in the pool that were in it at 9:00.

How many people got out of the pool?

Strategy hints!

1. Look for the important words in the question.
4. Use a table or a chart.
9. Think logically.

ISBN 978 1 4202 9396 8

COMPUTER VIRUS

A computer virus named Double Trouble is released. It destroys bytes on a computer's hard drive.

Each second, it wipes out twice the number of bytes that it did in the previous second.

This shows its destructive power:

Seconds	3	4	5	6
Bytes wiped	3	6	12	24

a) How many seconds will it be before the virus destroys over 1000 bytes per second?

b) How many bytes, in total, will the virus have destroyed after 2 seconds?

Extension

A computer virus named Triple Trouble is released.

Each second, it wipes out 3 times the number of bytes that it did in the previous second.

In the first second, it wipes out 1 byte. How many bytes, in total, will it have wiped out after 6 seconds?

Strategy hints!

1. Look for the important words in the question.
2. Look for a pattern.
4. Use a table or a chart.

ISBN 978 1 4202 9396 8

FIND THE NUMBERS

a) Find all the numbers less than 40 that are not in the 2 times table, 3 times table or 5 times table.

b) Find all the numbers between 60 and 80 that are not in the 2 times table, 3 times table or 7 times table.

Extension

a) Find all the numbers less than 50 that are not in the 2 times table, 3 times table, 5 times table, 7 times table or 11 times table.

b) Find all the numbers from 60 to 100 that are not in the 2 times table, 3 times table, 5 times table, 7 times table or 11 times table.

Strategy hints!

1 Look for the important words in the question.

2 Look for a pattern.

9 Think logically.

ISBN 978 1 4202 9396 8

NECTAR SEARCH

A butterfly flits from flower to flower in a special mathematical pattern as it searches for nectar.
It visits flowers 1, 2, 3, 5, 8 . . .

a) What will be the 8th flower that the butterfly visits?

b) How many flowers will the butterfly visit in this way before it flies past the 200th flower in the garden?

Extension

A gardener plants flowers in a circular pattern. The inner ring has 1 flower, the next ring has 4 flowers, the next ring has 16 flowers and so on. Which ring will have 4096 flowers?

Strategy hints!

1 Look for the important words in the question.

2 Look for a pattern.

4 Use a table or a chart.

ISBN 978 1 4202 9396 8

DIGIT FIND

a) Find all the 4-digit numbers, bigger than 8000, whose digits add up to 10.

b) Find the 8 smallest 4-digit numbers whose digits add up to a dozen.

Extension

a) Find all the 4-digit numbers, between 7000 and 7999, whose digits add up to 10.

b) Find the 8 biggest 4-digit numbers whose digits add up to an odd number smaller than 10.

Strategy hints!

1 Look for the important words in the question.

2 Look for a pattern.

9 Think logically.

ISBN 978 1 4202 9396 8

AGES AND AGES

My age multiplied by my mum's age equals 279 years.
Our ages add up to 40.

How old is Mum and how old am I?

Extension

My age added to my mum, my dad and my older sister's ages equals 86.
Dad was 24 when my sister was born.
Using my age and my mum's age from above, how old are my dad and my sister?

Strategy hints!

1 Look for the important words in the question.
3 Have a go.
9 Think logically.

ISBN 978 1 4202 9396 8

ARROWS OF CHANGE

These arrows change numbers: $\downarrow$ and $\leftarrow$

$40\downarrow = 8$ $\quad$ $100\downarrow = 20$

$9\leftarrow = 7$ $\quad$ $13\leftarrow = 11$

Find the answers to these problems:

a) $60\downarrow + 10\leftarrow - 30\downarrow = ?$

b) $20\downarrow \times 45\downarrow \times 12\leftarrow = ?$

Extension

Start at 631. What is the fewest number of arrows you can use to reach 1?

Strategy hints!

1. Look for the important words in the question.
2. Look for a pattern.
9. Think logically.

ISBN 978 1 4202 9396 8

FRANCO'S FRESH FISH

Franco's Fresh Fish is having a special on flathead.
The first 4 you buy cost $5 each.
The next 6 you buy cost $4 each.
The next 10 you buy cost $3 each.
All flatheads after this cost $2 each.

a) Mrs Brown bought 14 flatheads. How much did they cost?

b) Mr White spent $86 on flathead. How many did he buy?

Extension

When you buy 1 crayfish from Franco's, you get 4 prawns and 6 mussels for free.
Mr Green was having a crayfish party and took home 132 items.
How many of these items were free?

Strategy hints!

1. Look for the important words in the question.
9. Think logically.

ISBN 978 1 4202 9396 8

CRICKET GEAR

At the Perfect Pitch Cricket Shop, 1 cricket bat and 2 pairs of pads cost $115.
1 cricket bat and 5 pairs of pads cost $151.

a) How much does 1 bat cost?

b) How much does 1 pair of pads cost?

c) Our school bought 2 bats, 2 pairs of pads and 2 pairs of batting gloves from Perfect Pitch. The total cost was $224.

How much does 1 pair of batting gloves cost?

Extension

In cricket, you can score 1s, 2s, 3s, 4s and 6s.
Our best batter Megan scored a century last week in only 20 scoring shots. She only made 2 types of scores. One was odd and one was even.

What scoring shots did Megan make?

Strategy hints!

1. Look for the important words in the question.
2. Look for a pattern.
3. Have a go.

ISBN 978 1 4202 9396 8

SPLAT

In the game of Splat, 7 cards are turned face down on a table and a player selects 3 cards.
The cards are 1, 2, 3, 4, 5, x 2 and x 5.
Number cards are added up and the order of the cards does not matter.
So, a draw of 1, x 2, 3 would be added up like this:

$1 + 3 = 4 \qquad 4 \times 2 = 8$

Find all the different ways you could score 30 points in the game of Splat.

Extension

What is the smallest even number, after 4, that you could not possibly make in Splat?

Strategy hints!

1. Look for the important words in the question.
3. Have a go.
9. Think logically.

ISBN 978 1 4202 9396 8

HOOPLA

In the game of Hoopla, a player throws 3 rubber rings at numbered hooks on a board to try and score points. The hooks are numbered with all the odd numbers from 1 to 19. The order does not matter. So, a throw of 3, then 7, then 9 is the same as 7, then 9, then 3.

a) Find all the ways you can score a total of 9 points with 3 throws.
b) Find all the ways you can score a total of 10 points with 3 throws.
c) Find all the ways you can score a total of 21 points with 3 throws.

Extension

Find all the ways you can score a total of 51 points with 3 throws.

Strategy hints!

1 Look for the important words in the question.

3 Have a go.

9 Think logically.

ISBN 978 1 4202 9396 8

SAME NUMBER

a) The same number is taken away from 20, three times, like 20 – 5 – 5 – 5.
The result is 10.1
What was the number?

b) A different number is added to 25, four times, like 25 + 5 + 5 + 5 + 5.
The result is 39.4.
What was the number?

Extension

a) A number is divided into itself 3 times.
The result is 1000 times smaller than the number itself.
What was the number?

b) A number is multiplied by itself twice and then divided by 3.
The answer is 72.
What was the number?

Strategy hints!

1 Look for the important words in the question.

3 Have a go.

9 Think logically.

ISBN 978 1 4202 9396 8

FOOTBALL JUMPERS

The coach of the Lakeside Cougars sees 2 footballers standing next to each other with their backs to him.
He notices that the numbers on their jumpers, left to right, form a 3-digit number.
He also notices that if you multiply the number of the football jumper on the left by itself, you get the number of the football jumper on the right.

Which possible numbers could be on the football jumpers?

Extension

In Australian Rules football, a goal is worth 6 points and a behind is worth 1 point.
At the end of a game, the Falcons had kicked twice as many goals as behinds and had scored 91 points in total.
How many goals and how many behinds did the Falcons kick?

Strategy hints!

1. Look for the important words in the question.
3. Have a go.
9. Think logically.

ISBN 978 1 4202 9396 8

SCREEN CODE

The screen code in a calculator determines which of the 7 light bars will turn on when you type a digit.

4 is shown in this way:

Light Bar	1	2	3	4	5	6	7
	Off	On	On	On	Off	On	Off

(Hint: Light bar 1 is at the top, light bar 2 is top left, light bar 3 is top right, light bar 4 is central, light bar 5 is bottom left, light bar 6 is bottom right and light bar 7 is at the bottom.)

a) Which digit is the only one shown with light bar 6 off?

b) Which digits are shown with light bar 4 off?

Extension

a) What is the biggest 2-digit number that is shown on a calculator with 7 light bars on and 7 light bars off?

b) What is the biggest 3-digit number that is shown with $\frac{2}{3}$ of the possible light bars on and $\frac{1}{3}$ off?

Strategy hints!

1 Look for the important words in the question.

3 Have a go.

5 Use a drawing.

ISBN 978 1 4202 9396 8

SOFT TOYS

There are 8 types of soft toy pets for sale in the Cuddly Animal toyshop.

a) Find all the ways you can spend $12 to buy 3 soft toy pets.

b) Find all the ways you can spend $20 to buy 3 soft toy pets.

Extension

Make up more problems like this one. See if a classmate can work them out.

Strategy hints!

1. Look for the important words in the question.
2. Look for a pattern.
3. Have a go.

ISBN 978 1 4202 9396 8

DIFFERENT NUMBERS

A and B are 2 different numbers.

$A - B = 21$

$A \div B = 8$

Find the answer to these problems:

a) $A - (B \times B) = ?$

b) $(A + A + B) \div B = ?$

Extension

C and D are 2 different numbers.

Find the answer to this problem:

$\frac{C}{C} \times \frac{D}{D} + \frac{C}{C} + \frac{D}{D} = ?$

Strategy hints!

1 Look for the important words in the question.

3 Have a go.

7 Try an easier problem.

ISBN 978 1 4202 9396 8

PAINT THE FENCE

2 painters can paint 100 metres of fencing in an 8-hour day.

a) How long will it take 6 painters to paint 600 metres of fencing?
b) How long will it take 1 painter to paint 50 metres of fencing?

Extension

3 L of paint will be used for every 16 m of fence.
Basil the painter buys his paint in 10 L cans.

How many cans of paint will he need to paint 2 coats of paint on a fence that is 141 m long?

Strategy hints!

1. Look for the important words in the question.
5. Use a drawing.
9. Think logically.

ISBN 978 1 4202 9396 8

HEALTHY TUM

At the Healthy Tum Café, 2 gourmet sandwiches and 1 cup of coffee cost $9.60 altogether.
2 gourmet sandwiches cost 3 times as much as 1 coffee.

How much does 1 gourmet sandwich cost?

Extension

At the Healthy Tum Café, 1 protein milkshake and 2 health bars cost $6.80 altogether.
1 protein milkshake costs $4.40 more than 1 health bar.
How much does 1 protein milkshake cost?

Strategy hints!

1. Look for the important words in the question.
3. Have a go.
9. Think logically.

ISBN 978 1 4202 9396 8

NUMBER SEARCH

I am a 4-digit number with a 1-digit decimal.
My digits are 3, 3, 4, 6 and 8.
Rounded to the nearest 1000, I would equal 6000.
My larger 3 is 1000 times bigger than my smaller 3.
My 10s digit equals 2 multiplied by itself.

What number am I?

Extension

Make up a problem like this using a 4-digit number with a 1-digit decimal. See if a classmate can work it out.

Strategy hints!

1 Look for the important words in the question.

3 Have a go.

9 Think logically.

ISBN 978 1 4202 9396 8

TRIPLE SQUARES

A triple square is a 3-digit number.
In triple squares, all 3 digits are different. All 3 digits are the result of multiplying a number by itself.
For example, 1 x 1 = 1, 2 x 2 = 4 and 3 x 3 = 9, so 149 is a triple square.

Find all the other triple squares.

Extension

A near triple square is a 3-digit number that has 3 different digits. All of the digits are 1 away from a number that is the result of multiplying a number by itself.
For example, 2 is a digit that can be used, because it is next to 1.
There are 24 near triple squares.
Find all 24.

Strategy hints!

1. Look for the important words in the question.
2. Look for a pattern.
9. Think logically.

ISBN 978 1 4202 9396 8

MAKE A SUM

You can use four 4s and the 4 operation signs +, −, x and ÷ to make sums that equal many different answers.

For example:

4 x 4 + 4 + 4 = 24

Use four 4s, along with +, −, x or ÷ signs to create sums that equal these answers:

a) 16 **c)** 2

b) 0 **d)** 43

Extension

a) Use five 4s, along with +, −, x or ÷ signs to create a sum that equals 107.

b) Then, make up more problems like these ones. See if a classmate can work them out.

Strategy hints!

1 Look for the important words in the question.

3 Have a go.

9 Think logically.

ISBN 978 1 4202 9396 8

LIGHTNING LAD

Lightning Lad is a greyhound who loves to run. One day his owner Terry took him to a circular track for some exercise.

Lightning Lad started at point A and ran in a clockwise direction. He stopped for a rest at the 47th point he reached.

At which point on the track did Lightning Lad stop?

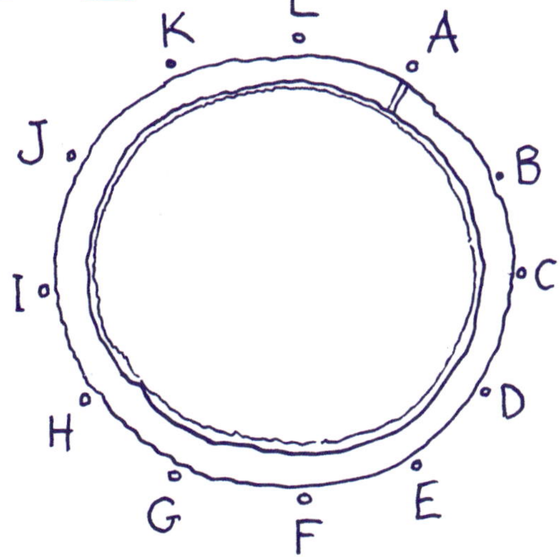

Extension

After a rest, Terry led Lightning Lad to point H and let him run around in an anticlockwise direction. This time Lightning Lad stopped for a rest at the 100th point he reached.

At which point on the track did Lightning Lad stop?

Strategy hints!

1. Look for the important words in the question.
2. Look for a pattern.
4. Use a table or a chart.

ISBN 978 1 4202 9396 8

QUARTERS AND HALVES

Andrew starts at 0 and skip counts upwards by $\frac{1}{4}$s.
Beth starts at 40 and skip counts downwards by 1s.

Which number will they both say at the same time?

Extension

Miranda starts at 0 and skip counts upwards by $\frac{1}{4}$s.
Gavin starts at 40 and skip counts downwards by $\frac{1}{2}$s.
They will not say the same number at the same time, but they will get very close.
What are the closest numbers that Miranda and Gavin will reach in this game?

Strategy hints!

1 Look for the important words in the question.
2 Look for a pattern.
4 Use a table or a chart.

ISBN 978 1 4202 9396 8

POSTIE NAT

Postie Nat delivers mail between Snake Island and Verity. Halfway between Snake Island and Verity is the town of Underbite. Halfway between Snake Island and Underbite is the town of Turgid.

It is 28.8 kilometres from Snake Island to Verity.

a) How far is it from Turgid to Verity?

b) Each day, Postie Nat has to drive from Snake Island to Turgid and back, then Snake Island to Underbite and back and finally Snake Island to Verity and back.

How far does Postie Nat drive in a day?

Extension

For every 7 letters in Postie Nat's bag, there is 1 magazine. For every 13 letters, there is 1 parcel.

What is the smallest number of items Postie Nat could have in her bag?

Strategy hints!

1 Look for the important words in the question.

4 Use a table or a chart.

5 Use a drawing.

ISBN 978 1 4202 9396 8

BUYING STAMPS

At a post office, stamps cost either 15 cents or 60 cents each and envelopes cost 5 cents each.

a) Tahlia wanted to buy an equal number of 15 cent stamps, 60 cent stamps and envelopes. She had $10.
How many of each stamp could she buy?

b) How much change would she have left over?

c) The following week, Tahlia bought twice as many 15 cent stamps as 60 cent stamps and an envelope for every stamp. The total cost was $10.50.
How many envelopes did Tahlia buy?

Extension

At the post office, it costs $1.20 to post any parcel, plus 35 cents for every 100 grams the parcel weighs. Tahlia posted a parcel that cost her $3.65.
How much did the parcel weigh?

Strategy hints!

1 Look for the important words in the question.
2 Look for a pattern.
4 Use a table or a chart.

ISBN 978 1 4202 9396 8

DOG, CAT AND HORSE

In a day, a dog eats 3 times what a cat eats, and a cat eats $\frac{1}{40}$ of what a horse eats.
A farmer carries a bucket with feed for the 3 animals out to the barn.
It weighs 8800 grams.

How much does the dog's food weigh?

Extension

The cat, dog and horse weigh 498 kg altogether.
The horse is 70 times heavier than the dog and the dog is 7 times heavier than the cat.

How much does the horse weigh?

Strategy hints!

1 Look for the important words in the question.

9 Think logically.

ISBN 978 1 4202 9396 8

GRANDFATHER CLOCK

A grandfather clock strikes every hour.

It strikes the same number of times as the hour that it is showing.

For example, it strikes 3 times for 3 o'clock.

a) Starting at one minute past midnight on Monday morning, how many times will it strike until it finishes striking at 3 pm on Tuesday?

b) Starting at one minute past midnight on Sunday morning, on what day will the clock strike for the 1000th time?

Extension

A different grandfather clock strikes the same number of times as the hour that it is showing. It also strikes once at a quarter past the hour, once at half past the hour and once at three quarters past the hour.

How many times will the clock strike in a day?

Strategy hints!

1. Look for the important words in the question.
2. Look for a pattern.
4. Use a table or a chart.

ISBN 978 1 4202 9396 8

LIGHT IT UP

a) Find all the numbers less than 100 that are shown by 4 or 6 light bars on a calculator.

b) Find all the numbers less than 100 that are shown by more than 11 light bars on a calculator.

Extension

a) Find all the numbers from 100 to 200 that are shown by 14 or more light bars on a calculator.

b) Find the biggest 4-digit number that is shown by 14 light bars on a calculator.

Strategy hints!

1 Look for the important words in the question.

2 Look for a pattern.

9 Think logically.

ISBN 978 1 4202 9396 8

WELL BATTED

In cricket, you can score 1s, 2s, 3s, 4s and 6s.
In his cricket game, Mikali scored 10 runs in only 3 scoring shots.

Find all the ways that Mikali could have made this score.
Hint: The order of the runs does not matter. A score of 2, 4 and 6 is the same as a score of 6, 4 and 2.

Extension

The following week, Mikali scored 22 runs in only 5 scoring shots.

Find all the ways that Mikali could have made this score, if the order of the runs does not matter.

Strategy hints!

1 Look for the important words in the question.

3 Have a go.

ISBN 978 1 4202 9396 8

MULTIPLY

The symbol ! means to multiply a number by every whole number less than it.
For example, 3 ! means 3 x 2 x 1.

Find the answers to these problems:

a) 5 ! – 4 ! = ?

b) 5 ! ÷ 3 ! = ?

Extension

a) Which 2 numbers, when the symbol ! is put after them, do not change in size?

b) Which number becomes 120 times bigger when ! is put after it?

Strategy hints!

1 Look for the important words in the question.

9 Think logically.

ISBN 978 1 4202 9396 8

ROUND ROBIN

The Swifts, the Sharks and the Scorpions played against each other in a series of 3 games as part of a netball round robin. 79 goals were scored in total.
At the end of the round robin, the Swifts had scored 7 goals more than the Sharks and the Scorpions, who had each scored the same number of goals.

a) How many goals did each team score?

b) Lara, who played for the Scorpions, was voted most valuable player. She had scored $\frac{2}{3}$ of the Scorpions' goals.
How many goals had Lara scored?

Extension

In the netball championship, 8 teams played in a round robin arrangement.

How many matches were played?

Strategy hints!

1 Look for the important words in the question.

3 Have a go.

4 Use a table or a chart.

ISBN 978 1 4202 9396 8

STARTING POINT

a) A number is divided by 2 and the result is then divided by 3. The answer is 17.
What is the starting number?

b) A number has 10 removed from it, then it is halved, and then it is multiplied by 5.
The answer is 5.
What is the starting number?

Extension

A number is tripled, then 8 is taken away from it, and then it is divided by 2. The answer is 35.

What is the starting number?

Strategy hints!

1. Look for the important words in the question.
3. Have a go.
6. Work backwards.

ISBN 978 1 4202 9396 8

PLUMBER'S BILL

Bill the plumber charges \$25 for 15 minutes, \$40 for 30 minutes, \$50 for 45 minutes or \$60 for an hour.
Bill laid some pipes for Mr Waters and recorded the hours he worked.
How much did Mr Waters have to pay Bill?

Day	Time worked
Monday	1 hour 30 minutes
Tuesday	3 hours
Wednesday	2 hours 15 minutes
Thursday	45 minutes
Friday	1 hour 15 minutes

Extension

Liz the plumber has a special billing method. If you pay with cash, she gives you a $\frac{1}{10}$ discount. If you pay with a cheque, you pay the full amount. If you pay by post, Liz adds $\frac{1}{10}$ to the bill.
Mr Piper paid by post. He was charged \$1210.

a) What was the bill before the $\frac{1}{10}$ was added?

b) How much would Mr Piper have saved if he had paid with cash?

Strategy hints!

1 Look for the important words in the question.
3 Have a go.
9 Think logically.

ISBN 978 1 4202 9396 8

BY ITSELF

A number is multiplied by itself. The answer is the same as if the number was multiplied by 10 and then 21 was taken away from it.

What is the starting number?

Extension

A number is multiplied by itself, and then multiplied by itself again. The answer is the same as if the number was multiplied by 10 and then added to itself 6 times.

What is the starting number?

Strategy hints!

1 Look for the important words in the question.

3 Have a go.

9 Think logically.

ISBN 978 1 4202 9396 8

EXCHANGE RATE

Satoshi needs to travel to Japan for a meeting.
In Japan, they use yen and not dollars.
Satoshi needs to take 12 000 yen on his trip.

Exchange rate:
1 dollar = 60 Japanese yen

a) How much will this cost Satoshi in dollars when he changes his money?

b) If the value of the yen had dropped suddenly to 1 dollar = 80 Japanese yen, how many dollars would Satoshi save?

Extension

When Satoshi comes back from Japan, he still has 3600 yen. He changes these back into dollars. The exchange rate is 1 dollar = 80 Japanese yen.

The money changers take $\frac{1}{10}$ of the money in the deal and give Satoshi the rest.

How many dollars does Satoshi receive in the exchange?

Strategy hints!

- 1 Look for the important words in the question.
- 4 Use a table or a chart.
- 9 Think logically.

ISBN 978 1 4202 9396 8

MAXIMUM AND MINIMUM

The maximum and minimum temperatures for 3 cities were recorded on a day in April.

a) Which city had the biggest range of temperature change on the day? By how many degrees did it change?

b) What was the temperature midpoint for each city?

City	Minimum (degrees)	Maximum (degrees)
Eastville	4.7	21.3
Westville	17.1	31.5
Northville	23.4	33.2

Extension

Southville's maximum temperature for April is $\frac{1}{4}$ of the sum of the 3 cities' maximums from above.

What is Southville's average maximum temperature for April?

Strategy hints!

1. Look for the important words in the question.
4. Use a table or a chart.
9. Think logically.

ISBN 978 1 4202 9396 8

CHEEKY RABBIT

A cheeky rabbit went into a shopping centre and decided to play on the escalator. She hopped up the down escalator, 5 steps at a time, to see what would happen. She found that for every 5 steps she hopped up, the escalator moved her down 2 steps.

There were 50 steps on the escalator.

How many 5 hop moves did the rabbit take to reach the top step of the escalator?

Extension

When the weather became hot, the rabbit started to shed some hair from its paws.

Each paw was covered with 1000 tiny hairs. The rabbit needed to shed hair until there was only half that amount. Every day, the rabbit shed 10 hairs for every 3 new hairs she grew.

How many days did the shedding take?

Strategy hints!

1 Look for the important words in the question.

2 Look for a pattern.

4 Use a table or a chart.

ISBN 978 1 4202 9396 8

FIND MY NUMBER

I am a 4-digit number with a 1-digit decimal.
My number contains 1, 3, 4, 7 and 7.
One of my 7s is 100 times bigger than the other.
When I am rounded to the nearest 1000, I equal 4000.
When I am rounded to the nearest whole number, my whole number digits will not change.
My decimal has 2 light bars when shown on a calculator.

What number am I?

Extension

Use 1, 3, 4, 7 and 7 to make both the biggest and the 3rd biggest possible 4-digit numbers with single digit decimals. Find the difference between these 2 numbers.

Strategy hints!

1 Look for the important words in the question.

9 Think logically.

ISBN 978 1 4202 9396 8

DESCENDIGITAL NUMBERS

A descendigital number is one whose digits get smaller from left to right, like 631. The digits in a descendigital number are all different.

Find all the 4-digit descendigital numbers that are smaller than 5000.

Extension

a) Find all the 4-digit descendigital numbers in the 5000s.

b) Find all the 5-digit descendigital numbers in the 60 000s.

Strategy hints!

1. Look for the important words in the question.
2. Look for a pattern.
3. Have a go.

ISBN 978 1 4202 9396 8

SYMBOL SHIFTER

The symbol [#] changes numbers in a certain way.

5 [#] = 13 10 [#] = 28 1 [#] = 1

Find the answers to these problems:

a) 7 [#] = ?

b) 20 [#] [#] = ?

c) 4 [#] [#] [#] = ?

Extension

The symbol [∧] changes numbers in a certain way.

1 [∧] = 3 5 [∧] = 127 10 [∧] = 1002

Find the answers to these problems:

a) 4 [∧] – 3 [∧] = ?

b) 2 [∧] x 3 [∧] = ?

Strategy hints!

1. Look for the important words in the question.
2. Look for a pattern.
9. Think logically.

ISBN 978 1 4202 9396 8

GENEROUS GRAN

A generous gran decided to give away some of her money to her relatives.

She gave $\frac{1}{2}$ of her money to her grandson.

She gave $\frac{1}{2}$ of the money left to her son.

She gave $\frac{1}{3}$ of the money left to her cousin.

She gave $\frac{1}{4}$ of the money left to her niece.

She then had $30 left and went to the movies.

a) How much money did Gran start off with?

b) What fraction of the starting amount of money did each of the 4 relatives receive?

Extension

A generous friend decides to give away $32 000. To each friend, he gives away half of what he has left.

How many people will he give money to before he has $31.25 left?

Strategy hints!

1. Look for the important words in the question.
6. Work backwards.

ISBN 978 1 4202 9396 8

NUMBER LINE

A number line from 0 to 1 has been divided into twelfths from left to right. There are 5 points on the line called A, B, C, D and E.

- A is bigger than $\frac{3}{4}$
- B is to the left of C and it is smaller than $\frac{4}{12}$
- C is at $\frac{1}{2}$
- D is at $\frac{1}{3}$
- E is at $\frac{9}{12}$

List the points in order from left to right.

Extension

A different number line from 0 to 1 has been divided into tenths from left to right.

F is at $\frac{7}{10}$, G is at $\frac{1}{5}$, H is at $\frac{4}{5}$, I is at $\frac{1}{10}$ and J is at $\frac{1}{2}$.

a) List the points in order from left to right.

b) What is the sum of the 5 points?

Strategy hints!

1 Look for the important words in the question.

2 Look for a pattern.

5 Use a drawing.

ISBN 978 1 4202 9396 8

CIRCULAR LETTER PATTERN

A letter pattern begins like this: A, D, G . . .
When it gets past Z, it begins again and goes on through the alphabet until it starts repeating itself.

a) What is in position 16 in this pattern?

b) A is the first letter in the pattern and the first in the alphabet. It is in the correct number/letter position.

What is the next letter of the alphabet that is in its correct number/letter position in this pattern?

Extension

A different circular letter pattern begins like this:
A, B, D, H . . .
What will the 10th letter be?

Strategy hints!

1. Look for the important words in the question.
2. Look for a pattern.
8. Make a model.

ISBN 978 1 4202 9396 8

NO MORE SEVENS

If 7 disappeared, we would have to count like this:

1, 2, 3, 4, 5, 6, 8, 9 . . .

Any number containing a 7, like 97, or in the 7 times table, like 84, would have to disappear as well.

a) What would be the 50th number in this new number system?

b) What would be the first three 3-digit numbers to disappear?

Extension

If 2 and multiples of 2 disappeared instead of 7, how many numbers would be left up to 130?

Strategy hints!

1. Look for the important words in the question.
2. Look for a pattern.
4. Use a table or a chart.

ISBN 978 1 4202 9396 8

PILE UP

In the game of Pile Up, players take turns to put cards onto a pile or to take them away.

Alex and Madison are playing Pile Up.

1st move: Alex puts 4 cards onto the pile and Madison takes 1.

2nd move: Alex puts 4 cards onto the pile and Madison takes 2.

3rd move: Alex puts 4 cards onto the pile and Madison takes 3.

4th move: Alex puts 4 cards onto the pile and Madison takes 1 again.

a) After how many moves will the pile in the middle hold 21 cards?

b) There will never be 1 or 2 cards in the pile. At some point there will be 3, 4, 5, 6 and 7 cards in the pile but never 8. What is the 10th number of cards that will never be in the pile?

Extension

You have 8 cards in 2 piles. Pile A contains 1, 3, 5 and 7. Pile B contains 2, 4, 6 and 8. You put pile B under pile A and deal the cards out left, right, left, right and so on.

How many times do you need to do this before the piles are back where they started?

Strategy hints!

1 Look for the important words in the question.

2 Look for a pattern.

4 Use a table or a chart.

ISBN 978 1 4202 9396 8

PHONE BOOK

Louise Nichols opens a copy of the phone book for her city.
The book contains 300 pages. Each page contains 5 columns of names and about 100 names in each column.

a) Louise looks up her family's phone number. About $10\frac{1}{2}$ pages of the phone book have surnames starting with the letter N.
About how many surnames in the phone book start with the letter N?

b) Each name in the phone book represents about 3 people who use that phone number. About how many people live in Louise's city?

Extension

In a phone book, there are 10 Smiths for every 7 Williams, 4 Johnsons and 3 Nguyens. These names take up 264 columns in total.

How many columns are Johnsons?

Strategy hints!

1 Look for the important words in the question.

9 Think logically.

ISBN 978 1 4202 9396 8

READ ALL ABOUT IT

Today's copy of the *City Standard* newspaper contains 120 pages. 0.4 of the paper is advertisements. $\frac{1}{3}$ of the paper is sport. 0.1 of the paper is entertainment. The rest of the paper is news.

a) How many pages of the *City Standard* contain news?

b) Half of the news pages contain local news stories and half of the news pages contain overseas news stories.

What fraction of the paper is devoted to local news?

Extension

The *City Standard* varies in length each day, but its length is always a multiple of 4 pages. The Saturday paper is $\frac{1}{16}$ longer than the Sunday paper.

What is the shortest length that the Sunday paper could be?

Strategy hints!

1 Look for the important words in the question.

8 Make a model.

9 Think logically.

ISBN 978 1 4202 9396 8

HARRY'S BIRTHDAY

Today is Harry's birthday. He is celebrating it with his wife and 3 children. Only 1 of his children is still at school.
Harry's age contains 9 light bars on a calculator.
The digits of Harry's age differ by 2.
The 1s digit is bigger than the 10s digit in Harry's age.

What birthday is Harry celebrating?

Extension

The ages of Harry's 4 nephews add up to 19 and multiply to 198.
2 of the nephews are twins and they have a younger brother.
How old is Harry's oldest nephew?

Strategy hints!

1 Look for the important words in the question.

3 Have a go.

9 Think logically.

ISBN 978 1 4202 9396 8

Focus Number and place value
- Multiplication
- Division

BLURRED IMAGE

Anya prints an important 3-digit number, but the last digit does not print properly. She remembers that the 3-digit number was between 800 and 900, and was in both the 3 times table and the 4 times table.

What could the 3-digit number have been?

Extension

There is a very important year in history that is in both the 3 times table and the 4 times table. Which of the following years is it?

- 1788 – First Fleet arrives in Australia
- 1840 – Treaty of Waitangi, New Zealand
- 1912 – Sinking of the Titanic
- 1959 – Sir Edmund Hillary and Tenzing Norgay climb Mount Everest
- 1969 – First person walks on the moon

Strategy hints!

1 Look for the important words in the question.

3 Have a go.

9 Think logically.

ISBN 978 1 4202 9396 8

DIFFERENT DIGITS

A, B and C are 3 different digits. They are all whole numbers. They are all bigger than 1.

$$\begin{array}{r} AB \\ AB \\ +\ AB \\ \hline CB \\ \hline \end{array}$$

What numbers are A, B and C?

Extension

D and E are 2 different digits. They are both whole numbers.

$$\begin{array}{r} DE \\ \times\ \ E \\ \hline 144 \end{array}$$

What numbers are D and E? There are 2 possible answers.

Strategy hints!

1. Look for the important words in the question.
3. Have a go.
9. Think logically.

ISBN 978 1 4202 9396 8

ROSIE'S CARDS

Rosie has 4 cards numbered 2, 3 6 and 7.

a) Find all of the even, 3-digit numbers she could make with these cards.

b) Find all of the even, 4-digit numbers she could make with these cards.

Extension

Rosie has 5 cards numbered 1, 2, 3, 4 and 5.

a) Find all of the odd, 3-digit numbers from 200 to 400 that she could make with these cards.

b) Find all of the even, 4-digit numbers bigger than 3500 that she could make with these cards.

Strategy hints!

1 Look for the important words in the question.

2 Look for a pattern.

9 Think logically.

ISBN 978 1 4202 9396 8

LETTERBOXES

a) The number on my letterbox, when added to my 2 next door neighbours' letterbox numbers, equals 117.
What is my letterbox number?

b) The number on my nan's letterbox, when added to her 2 next door neighbours' letterbox numbers, equals 210.
What are the letterbox numbers of my nan's 2 next door neighbours?

Extension

My uncle lives in a fairly short street.
He lives on the even-numbered side of his street. There is an equal number of houses on both sides of his street.
The letterbox numbers on my uncle's side of the street add up to 182.
How many houses are in my uncle's street?

Strategy hints!

1. Look for the important words in the question.
2. Look for a pattern.
3. Have a go.

ISBN 978 1 4202 9396 8

LANDOPOLY

In the game of Landopoly, 1 block of land costs $5.
5 blocks of land cost the same as 1 flat. 5 flats cost the same as 1 apartment.
5 apartments cost the same as 1 house. 5 houses cost the same as 1 mansion.

a) How much does 1 mansion cost?

b) Last time I played Landopoly, I owned 6 pieces of property worth $890.
What did I own?

Extension

In a new version of Landopoly, the value of the properties is changed.
1 block of land costs $5. 10 blocks of land cost the same as 1 flat. 5 flats cost the same as 1 apartment. 10 apartments cost the same as 1 house. 5 houses cost the same as 1 mansion.

How much does 1 mansion cost in this version of the game?

Strategy hints!

1 Look for the important words in the question.

3 Have a go.

4 Use a table or a chart.

ISBN 978 1 4202 9396 8

DIVIDER'S DELIGHT

88 can be divided by 2 three times before it turns into a fraction.

$88 \div 2 = 44$ $44 \div 2 = 22$ $22 \div 2 = 11$ $11 \div 2 = 5\frac{1}{2}$

There is a 2-digit number that can be divided by 2 six times before it turns into a fraction.

What is that number?

Extension

What is the first 3-digit number that can be divided by 2 four times before it turns into a fraction?

Strategy hints!

1 Look for the important words in the question.

3 Have a go.

9 Think logically.

ISBN 978 1 4202 9396 8

LIGHTHOUSES

There are 3 dangerous rocky capes on the Surf Coast.
Each cape has a lighthouse that flashes at different times.
Cape Alfred flashes every 20 seconds.
Cape Norman flashes every 25 seconds.
Cape Winjira flashes every 30 seconds.

a) How often do all 3 lighthouses flash at the same time?

b) In the time it takes for all 3 lighthouses to flash at the same time, how often will 2 lighthouses flash together?

Extension

3 lights flash together every 165 seconds. One flashes every 3 seconds and another flashes every 5 seconds.

How often does the 3rd light flash?

Strategy hints!

1 Look for the important words in the question.

4 Use a table or a chart.

ISBN 978 1 4202 9396 8

CHESS PIECES

Chess is played on a square board that is 8 squares by 8 squares.
Each player starts the game with 16 pieces.

a) Sam and Jasmine are playing a game of chess.
Near the end of the game, only $\frac{1}{8}$ of the board contains pieces.
How many pieces have Sam and Jasmine lost altogether?

b) When Jasmine wins the game, she has her king, queen, 2 knights and 1 pawn left.
Sam only has his king.
What fraction of the board was covered with pieces when Jasmine called "Checkmate"?

Extension

A chess tournament involves 32 players in a knockout format. Every time a player wins a match, they progress to the next round. The losing player is knocked out of the competition.

How many matches will be played in the tournament?

Strategy hints!

1 Look for the important words in the question.

4 Use a table or a chart.

9 Think logically.

ISBN 978 1 4202 9396 8

MEASUREMENT AND GEOMETRY

BABY ELEPHANTS

There are 2 baby elephants at the city zoo. Zazu is 6 months old and Bazeri is 12 months old.

Together, they weigh exactly 1 tonne. Bazeri weighs 190 kilograms more than Zazu.

a) How much does each baby elephant weigh?

b) 6 months ago, Bazeri weighed what Zazu weighs now. The elephants will each grow to weigh about 5 tonnes as adults.

If Bazeri continues to grow at the same rate, about how old will she be when she reaches her full adult weight?

Extension

Together, the 4 rhinos at the zoo weigh 3.29 tonnes. Their weights all differ by the same amount.

The lightest rhino weighs 800 kg. What do the other 3 rhinos weigh?

Strategy hints!

1. Look for the important words in the question.
4. Use a table or a chart.

ISBN 978 1 4202 9396 8

DISTANCES

a) Charlie's house is 0.6 kilometres away from Amber's house. Finn's house is 1.0 kilometres away from Amber's house. Lucy's house is halfway between Finn's house and Charlie's house.

How far away is Lucy's house from Amber's house?

b) Jasmine, Tom, Harry and Natalie are standing in a line. Tom is 0.3 metres away from Jasmine. Harry is 1 metre away from Jasmine. Natalie is halfway between Tom and Harry.

How far apart are Natalie and Jasmine?

Extension

Mr Zeno fires an arrow at a target that is 64 m away from him.

What fraction of the distance has the arrow covered when it is 25 cm from the bull's eye?

Strategy hints!

1 Look for the important words in the question.

5 Use a drawing.

8 Make a model.

ISBN 978 1 4202 9396 8

FLIGHT TO PORTSVILLE

A flight from Morton to Portsville is about 3000 kilometres. 30 minutes into a flight, Portsville is 2625 kilometres away and the flight still has 3 hours to go.

How many kilometres per hour is the plane flying?

Extension

The plane leaves Morton at 11:25 am. Portsville is 2 hours behind Morton time.

The flight is 40 minutes late on arrival.

What is the time in Portsville when the plane lands?

Strategy hints!

1 Look for the important words in the question.

4 Use a table or a chart.

9 Think logically.

ISBN 978 1 4202 9396 8

SCALE TRAIL

On a map, 1 centimetre represents 25 kilometres.

a) The road trip from Westville to North Point is a distance of 331 kilometres. How many centimetres would represent this distance on the map?

b) How many millimetres would represent a distance of 10 kilometres on the map?

Extension

The distance between 2 towns is represented on a map by 4 mm. The real distance is 130 km.

How many kilometres does 1 cm represent on this map?

Strategy hints!

1 Look for the important words in the question.

8 Make a model.

9 Think logically.

ISBN 978 1 4202 9396 8

Focus Using units of measurement
- Perimeter
- Area

Measurement and Geometry 5

VEGIE PATCH

Carlo wants to make the biggest vegie patch that he can.
He has 24 one-metre long sleepers to use as a boundary.

a) What is the biggest possible vegie patch that Carlo can make with his 24 sleepers?

b) What is the second biggest possible vegie patch that Carlo can make if he cannot cut any of the sleepers?

Extension

a) What is the biggest possible vegie patch that Carlo can make with 80 sleepers that are each 50 cm long?

b) What is the biggest possible vegie patch that Carlo can make with 40 sleepers that are each 20 cm long?

Strategy hints!

1 Look for the important words in the question.

5 Use a drawing.

8 Make a model.

ISBN 978 1 4202 9396 8

RIGHT-ANGLED CLOCK

At 3:00, the hands on a clock face form a right angle.

How many times will the hands form a right angle between 2:55 am and 8:00 am?
Hint: The times may fall in between two minutes.

Extension

At 12:00, the hands on a clock face form a straight line.
When are the next 10 times that this will happen?
Hint: The times may fall in between two minutes.

Strategy hints!

1 Look for the important words in the question.

5 Use a drawing.

8 Make a model.

ISBN 978 1 4202 9396 8

BOZO TURNS

Bozo the clown is in a circular ring.

The lion cage is in front of him. The trapeze is behind him. The snack bar is to his right. The jugglers are to his left.

a) Bozo starts to turn clockwise for $3\frac{3}{8}$ turns. Then he falls down.
Bozo is now between 2 things. What are they?

b) Bozo gets up. He keeps facing the same direction. Then, he turns anticlockwise until he sees the jugglers for the 4th time.
He falls down again.
How many turns did Bozo make to be in this position?

Extension

You are facing north. You turn $\frac{1}{8}$ of a turn clockwise, then $\frac{1}{4}$ of a turn anticlockwise, then $\frac{3}{8}$ of a turn clockwise, and so on in this pattern.

After how many turns will you be facing south for the 2nd time?

Strategy hints!

1 Look for the important words in the question.

5 Use a drawing.

ISBN 978 1 4202 9396 8

CURIOUS ANT

A curious ant looks up at a square-based pyramid. It decides to crawl along every edge of the pyramid, trying not to go over each edge more than once, if it can.

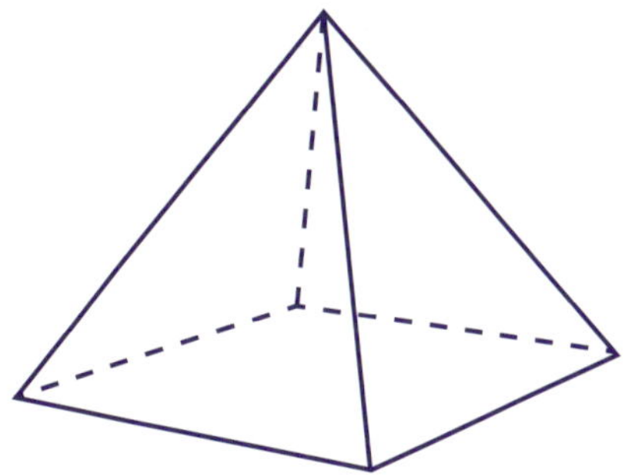

a) What is the smallest number of edges that the ant must crawl along to do this?

b) Each edge of this square-based pyramid is 5.5 centimetres long.

How far will the ant crawl in its exploration?

Extension

The total length of all the edges of a different square-based pyramid is 102 cm.
The edges of the base of this pyramid are all 10 cm long.

How long is each of its other edges?

Strategy hints!

1 Look for the important words in the question.

5 Use a drawing.

8 Make a model.

ISBN 978 1 4202 9396 8

ALL THE SQUARES

How many squares can you see in the picture?

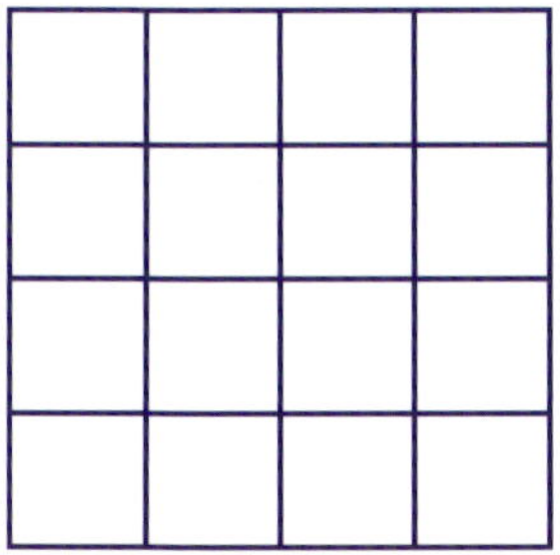

Extension

How many squares can you see in the picture?

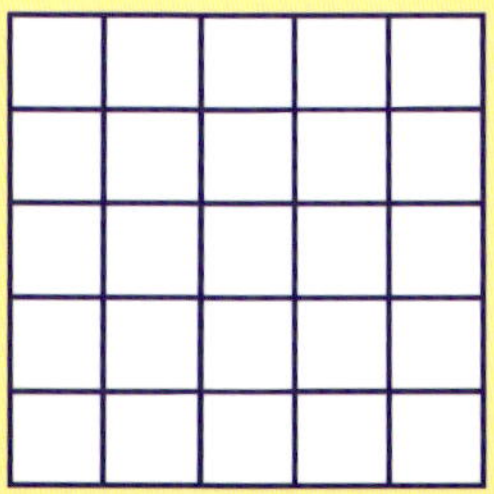

Strategy hints!

1. Look for the important words in the question.
2. Look for a pattern.
5. Use a drawing.

ISBN 978 1 4202 9396 8

WASHING DAY

Mr Smedley does his washing every Saturday. His washing machine holds 45 litres of water. After filling and washing, it then goes into a rinse part of the cycle. For 2 minutes, the machine spins and then fills with fresh water at the same time. As it spins, it loses 10 litres a minute and it fills at the rate of 5 litres a minute.

a) 30 seconds into the rinse cycle, how much water is in the machine?

b) Mr Smedley's washing machine fills, rinses for 2 minutes, empties, fills again, then empties in a full cycle.

How much water does this cycle use?

Extension

After the spin cycle of a washing machine, the clothes in the machine still have the equivalent of $1\frac{1}{2}$ L of water in them. The wet washing is put into a basket weighing 850 g. The basket, when full of washing, weighs 4.7 kg.

What will the clothes weigh when they are dry?

Strategy hints!

1 Look for the important words in the question.

4 Use a table or a chart.

ISBN 978 1 4202 9396 8

WHERE IN LINE?

Anna, Ben, Carlos, David, Eric, Frank, Gita and Harry are in a line.
Anna is next to Ben.
Gita has 2 people to her right.
There are 3 people between Harry and Gita.
Frank has no-one to his right.
Harry is next to Anna.
Eric is to the right of Carlos and to the left of David.

List the students from left to right.

Strategy hints!

1 Look for the important words in the question.
5 Use a drawing.
8 Make a model.

Extension

Make up more problems like this one. See if a classmate can work them out.

ISBN 978 1 4202 9396 8

HORIZONTAL AND VERTICAL

a) What are the first three odd, 2-digit numbers made up of 5 vertical light bars and 4 horizontal light bars on a calculator?

b) What are the first four 2-digit numbers made up of 5 vertical light bars and 1 horizontal light bar on a calculator?

Extension

a) What is the biggest 3-digit number made up of 3 horizontal light bars and 6 vertical light bars on a calculator?

b) What is the 2nd smallest 4-digit number made up of 3 horizontal light bars and 8 vertical light bars on a calculator?

Strategy hints!

1 Look for the important words in the question.

3 Have a go.

5 Use a drawing.

ISBN 978 1 4202 9396 8

Focus Using units of measurement
- Speed
- Time

TRAVEL TIMES

A turtle can walk 1 metre in 10 seconds.
An athlete can run 100 metres in 10 seconds.
A bullet train can travel 1 kilometre in 10 seconds.

a) How many metres, in total, will all 3 travel in 1 second?
b) How many metres, in total, will all 3 travel in 1 minute?

Extension

A train travelling at 60 km per hour travels south towards another train that is travelling north at 100 km per hour. They are 20 km apart.

How far apart will they be half an hour later?

Strategy hints!

1 Look for the important words in the question.

4 Use a table or a chart.

ISBN 978 1 4202 9396 8

TWELVE HOURS

Imagine what would happen if the government decided that there would only be 12 hours in a day instead of 24.

a) How many old time minutes would be in the new time of $2\frac{1}{4}$ hours?

b) How many old time minutes would be in the new time of $5\frac{1}{2}$ hours?

Extension

a) What old time would equal the new time of 4:43?

b) What old time would equal the new time of 2:35?

Strategy hints!

1. Look for the important words in the question.
4. Use a table or a chart.
9. Think logically.

ISBN 978 1 4202 9396 8

DIVIDED RECTANGLE

A rectangle is divided from corner to corner and midpoint to midpoint.

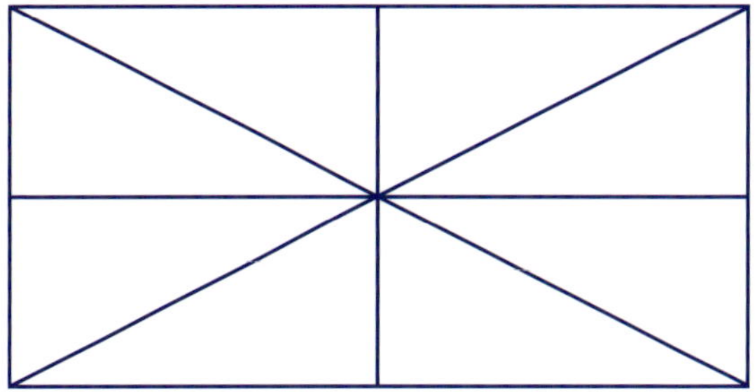

a) How many right angles can be found in the changed rectangle?

b) How many angles less than a right angle can be found in the changed rectangle?

Extension

Look at the shape above.

a) How many triangles can be found in the changed rectangle?

b) Lines are drawn from the midpoint of each of the rectangle's edges to form a new shape. What shape is formed?

c) How many triangles can be found in the shape from part **b)**?

Strategy hints!

1 Look for the important words in the question.

5 Use a drawing.

ISBN 978 1 4202 9396 8

HOLLOW CUBE

Billy makes a big hollow cube from
24 smaller cubes.
Then, Billy paints every face blue.

How many faces does Billy paint?

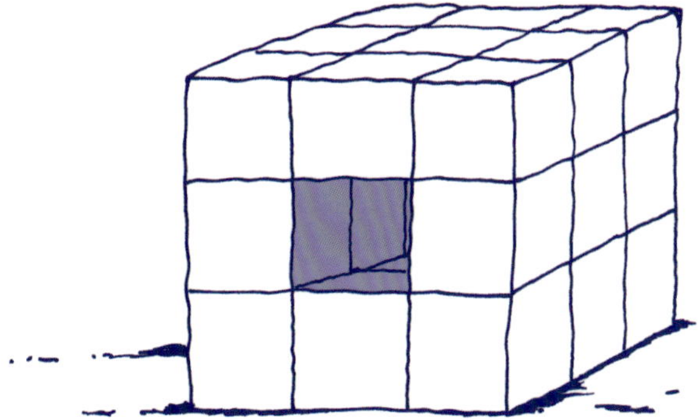

Extension

How many edges and vertices (corners) does the hollow cube have?

Strategy hints!

1 Look for the important words in the question.

5 Use a drawing.

8 Make a model.

ISBN 978 1 4202 9396 8

THREE VEHICLES

There are some plastic vehicles in Toby's toy box.
The buses weigh 12 grams each, the trucks weigh 8 grams each and the cars weigh 4 grams each.
Toby gets an equal number of each type of vehicle. He wants his vehicles to weigh as close to 1 kilogram as possible.

How many of each vehicle will Toby collect?

Extension

Toby has twice the number of cars as trucks, and twice the number of trucks as buses. He weighs the vehicles and finds that he is as close to 100 g as he can be with this combination.

How many vehicles does Toby have altogether?

Strategy hints!

1 Look for the important words in the question.

4 Use a table or a chart.

9 Think logically.

ISBN 978 1 4202 9396 8

PAPER FOLDING

Emma holds an A4 piece of paper landscape and folds it in half from left edge to right edge.
Then, she folds it in half from top to bottom.
Then, she folds it in half from left edge to right edge.
Then, Emma unfolds the paper and counts all the right angles.

How many right angles does Emma count?

Extension

After unfolding the paper, Emma draws a diagonal line from the top right corner to the bottom left corner of the paper. This makes a triangle, which Emma then cuts out.

How many right angles are there on this triangle?

Strategy hints!

1. Look for the important words in the question.
5. Use a drawing.
8. Make a model.

ISBN 978 1 4202 9396 8

SPLIT HEXAGON

A hexagon has had its corners joined to form 6 equal sections, numbered 1 to 6.

a) Which sections can be joined to form a rhombus?

b) Which sections can be joined to form a trapezoid?

c) Which individual sections are equilateral triangles?

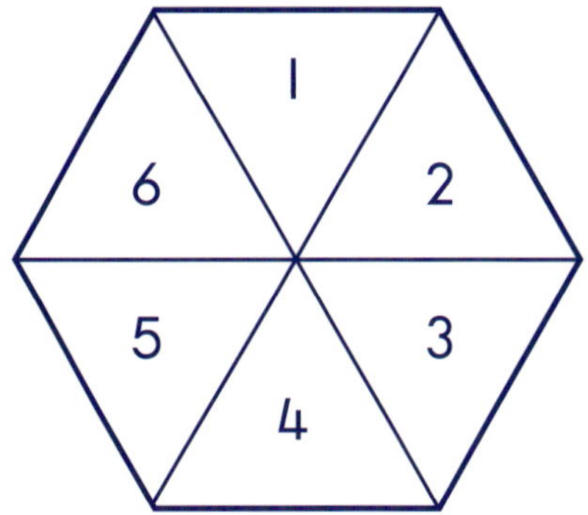

Extension

The midpoints of sections 1 and 4 are joined.

a) How many right angles can now be found in the hexagon?

b) How many angles smaller than a right angle can now be found in the hexagon?

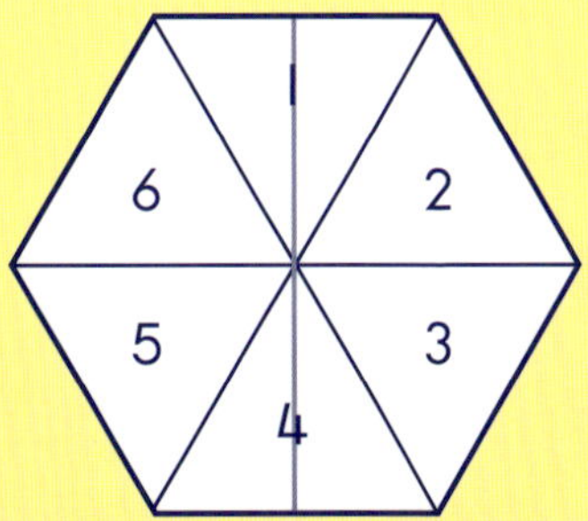

Strategy hints!

1 Look for the important words in the question.

5 Use a drawing.

ISBN 978 1 4202 9396 8

RAINY DAYS

We had exactly 1 metre of rain last year.

The rainfall from January to June was 7 times the rainfall from July to December.

How much rain fell in each half of the year?

Extension

a) There was 190 mm of rain in June but only 231 mm for the whole of winter.

Using the information from above, how much rain fell between September and December last year?

b) The rainfall in September was 3 times the rainfall in October, and the rainfall in October was 3 times the rainfall in November.

There was only 6 mm of rain in December.

How much rain fell in September? How much fell in October? How much fell in November?

Strategy hints!

1. Look for the important words in the question.
4. Use a table or a chart.
9. Think logically.

ISBN 978 1 4202 9396 8

FULL OF WATER

1 litre of water weighs 1 kilogram.

1 litre of water occupies the same space or volume as a 1000 MAB block.

a) How many millilitres of water will fill a rectangular tank that is 10 centimetres long, 5 centimetres wide and 4 centimetres high?

b) What is the weight of water that will fill a 20 centimetre by 20 centimetre by 20 centimetre tank?

Extension

A tap drips at a constant rate of 5 drips per minute. It takes 5 drips to make 4 mL of water.

An empty bucket that can hold 4 L of water is put under the tap.

How long will it take to fill the bucket?

Strategy hints!

1 Look for the important words in the question.

5 Use a drawing.

8 Make a model.

ISBN 978 1 4202 9396 8

PACKING BOXES

A cubical box is 1 metre long on all of its 12 edges.
Blocks of wood are being stacked inside it.
Each block is 1 metre long, 25 centimetres wide and 25 centimetres high.

How many will fit inside the box?

Extension

The container in which the filled cubical boxes are to be stored is 7 m long, $2\frac{1}{2}$ m high and $3\frac{1}{2}$ m wide.
How many filled cubical boxes will fit inside the container?

Strategy hints!

1. Look for the important words in the question.
5. Use a drawing.
9. Think logically.

ISBN 978 1 4202 9396 8

ALPHABETICAL MOVE

Mrs Thomas is hanging groups of 4 letters on hooks. She needs to hang them up in alphabetical order.

The letters are P M B T.

Every time Mrs Thomas swaps one letter on a hook for another, it is a 'move'.

Each letter can only be swapped with a letter that is next to it.

How many moves will Mrs Thomas make before the letters are in alphabetical order?

Extension

The next 4 letters Mrs Thomas has to put into order are W J C R.

How many moves will Mrs Thomas make before these letters are in alphabetical order?

Strategy hints!

1. Look for the important words in the question.
8. Make a model.
9. Think logically.

ISBN 978 1 4202 9396 8

FRACTIONAL TIME

a) What fraction of a decade is a week?

b) What fraction of $5\frac{1}{2}$ years is a month?

Extension

a) What fraction of 2 years is a fortnight?

b) What fraction of a century is 1 January to 30 June?

Strategy hints!

1. Look for the important words in the question.
4. Use a table or a chart.
7. Try an easier problem.

ISBN 978 1 4202 9396 8

SQUARES FROM SQUARES

4 squares of the same size can be combined together to form a larger square.

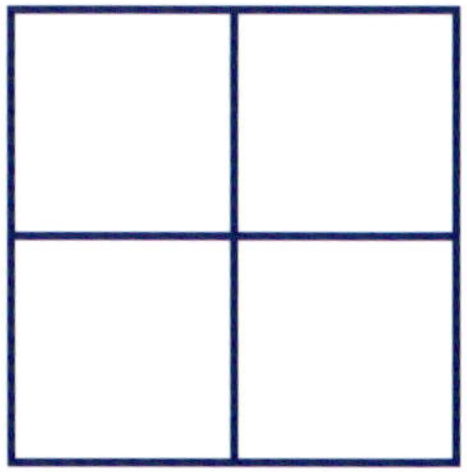

How many squares will be found in the next 3 larger squares that are made this way?

Extension

8 cubes of the same size can be connected together to form a larger cube.

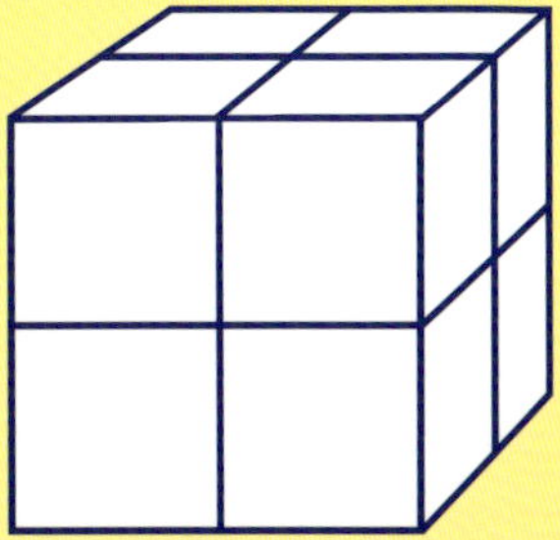

How many cubes will be found in the next 3 larger cubes that are made this way?

Strategy hints!

1 Look for the important words in the question.

5 Use a drawing.

8 Make a model.

ISBN 978 1 4202 9396 8

STATISTICS AND PROBABILITY

SPINNING WHEEL

Benjy goes to the fair and sees a spinning wheel. The wheel contains 20 numbers and offers 3 prizes. Benjy buys 3 tickets and watches as the 1st and 2nd prizes are won by tickets that he does not have.

a) What is Benjy's chance of winning the 3rd prize?

b) Benjy watches as the wheel is spun 9 times. The 3 winning ticket numbers are 4, 18 and 12.

What was the chance that all three 1st place ticket numbers would be even?

Extension

A lucky dip box has 20 tickets in it numbered 1 to 20.

How many tickets do you need to take out of the box to be guaranteed that at least 1 is an even number?

Strategy hints!

1 Look for the important words in the question.

9 Think logically.

ISBN 978 1 4202 9396 8

DIFFERENT COLOURS

9 plastic shells are put into a box. 3 are red, 3 are yellow and 3 are green.

a) Maria predicts that she will take out a green shell. What is her chance of being correct?

b) The shell is red. This red shell stays out of the box.
Maria predicts that the next shell will be green. What is her chance of being correct?

c) The shell is yellow. This yellow shell stays out of the box.
Maria predicts that the next shell will be green. What is her chance of being correct?

Extension

16 small plastic aeroplanes are put into a bag. 5 are green, 4 are red, 4 are blue and 3 are yellow.

What is the smallest number of planes that you need to take out of the box to guarantee that you have at least 1 of every coloured plane?

Strategy hints!

1. Look for the important words in the question.
8. Make a model.
9. Think logically.

ISBN 978 1 4202 9396 8

BASKETBALL BLITZ

In 6 basketball games, Miranda averaged 10 goals per game.

In game 1, she scored 4 goals.

In game 2, she scored 12 goals.

In game 3, she scored 5 goals.

a) How many goals must Miranda have scored in games 4 to 6?

b) After game 7, Miranda's goal average went up to 11 per game. How many goals must Miranda have scored in game 7?

Extension

Hannah scored 47 for her 5 spelling tests. Each test was out of 10.

If you removed her worst performance on any test, her average would have been 9.75.

How many 10 out of 10s did Hannah score?

Strategy hints!

1 Look for the important words in the question.

9 Think logically.

ISBN 978 1 4202 9396 8

HAIR AND SHOES

There are 42 students in our class.
Some of the students were surveyed to see if the shoes they wore on a certain day matched their hair colour.

	Black hair	Brown hair
Black shoes	11	6
Brown shoes	13	8

a) What does the fraction $\frac{1}{2}$ have to do with the survey?

b) What does the fraction $\frac{19}{21}$ have to do with the survey?

Extension

a) Using the table above, what is the biggest possible number of students in the class whose shoes and hair, on the day of the survey, might have matched?

b) What is the biggest possible number of students in the class whose shoes and hair, on the day of the survey, might not have matched?

Strategy hints!

1 Look for the important words in the question.

4 Use a table or a chart.

9 Think logically.

ISBN 978 1 4202 9396 8

DICE ROLL

Zoe rolls two 6-sided dice.

a) How many different combinations can she make with the 2 dice? Remember, a roll of 4 and 6 is different to a roll of 6 and 4.

b) What is the chance that she will roll a total of 4 or lower with the 2 dice?

c) What is the chance that she will roll a total that starts with the letter ‘T’ with the 2 dice?

d) What is the chance that she will roll a total that is in the 3 times table with the 2 dice?

Extension

Nathan rolls two 6-sided dice. One is red and one is blue.

a) What is the chance that the red die will roll a higher number than the blue die?

b) What is the chance that Nathan will roll numbers that add up to a total of 6, 7 or 8 with the 2 dice?

Strategy hints!

1 Look for the important words in the question.

4 Use a table or a chart.

ISBN 978 1 4202 9396 8

TRAINSPOTTING CHAMPIONS

The names of the top 120 trainspotters were recorded in a pie chart. There were representatives from Acton, Bartley, Cox, Dunbah, Echo Hill and Flynn.

How many of the top 120 came from either Acton or Cox?

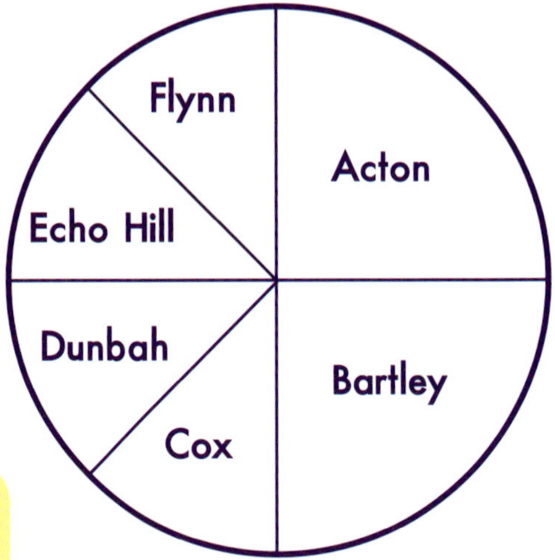

Extension

The top 10 received awards of excellence and 1 other was selected at random to win the Choo Choo Cup trophy.

6 of the top 10 were from Flynn.

Using the chart from above, what was the chance that the winner of the Choo Choo Cup trophy would also come from Flynn?

Strategy hints!

1 Look for the important words in the question.

4 Use a table or a chart.

9 Think logically.

ISBN 978 1 4202 9396 8

DIGIT CHANCE

Joshua is given 3 cards. They are 1, 7 and 2.

He is then asked to make as many different 3-digit numbers as he can using these 3 cards.

Sasha is asked to call out one of the 3-digit numbers Joshua has made.

What is the chance that the number Sasha calls out is even?

Extension

Joshua is then given 4 cards. They are 2, 5, 4 and 6.

This time he is asked to make as many different even, 4-digit numbers as he can using these 4 cards.

Sasha is asked to call out one of the 4-digit numbers Joshua has made.

What is the chance that the number Sasha calls out ends in a 4?

Strategy hints!

1. Look for the important words in the question.
4. Use a table or a chart.
9. Think logically.

ISBN 978 1 4202 9396 8

DAYS OF CHANCE

A newsagent is having a big clean up.
He is getting rid of old individual day calendars, some of which go back many years.
One page falls from its pad and is picked up by the newsagent.

What is the chance that the page is for a day in May?
There are 2 possible answers.

Extension

The newsagent picks up a page that has fallen from a different pad.

a) What is the chance that this page is from a day in spring?

b) What is the chance that this page is 7 October? There are 2 possible answers.

Strategy hints!

1 Look for the important words in the question.

9 Think logically.

ISBN 978 1 4202 9396 8

AVERAGE PERFORMANCE

5 whole numbers average 8.
1 of the numbers is 3 below average and
1 of the numbers is 3 above average.

What is the biggest that any one of the other 3 numbers could be?

Extension

5 different whole numbers average 8.
All the numbers are different.

What is the biggest possible difference that there could be between the biggest number and the second biggest number?

Strategy hints!

1. Look for the important words in the question.
9. Think logically.

ISBN 978 1 4202 9396 8

DECKS OF CARDS

2 decks of playing cards, with the jokers removed, are shuffled and then put into a pile in the middle of a table.

What is the chance of taking a card and it being a black ace?

Extension

2 decks of playing cards, with the jokers removed, are shuffled and then put into a pile in the middle of a table. 4 cards are removed from the deck. They are 10, jack, queen and king.

What is the chance of taking the top card and it being:

a) Another 10?

b) An even-numbered card?

c) A red odd-numbered card? Hint: The ace = 1.

Strategy hints!

1 Look for the important words in the question.

4 Use a table or a chart.

9 Think logically.

ISBN 978 1 4202 9396 8

ANSWERS

Number and Algebra

Answers 1

1. **Golf game**: **a)** Four 4s; **b)** Eight 4s and four 5s
(Hint: **a)** 33 – 5 = 28 and (4 x 4) + (4 x 3) = 28;
b) 70 – 18 = 62; (8 x 4) + (4 x 5) = 62)
Extension: 86 (4 x 6 = 24 and
(2 x 3) + (4 x 4) + (8 x 5) + 24 = 86)

2. **Numbers**: **a)** 84; **b)** 5 and 13
(Hint: **a)** 7 and 12 differ by 5; **b)** 5 x 13 = 65)
Extension: 4, 7, 10

3. **Starting number**: **a)** 2; **b)** 7
(Hint: **a)** 2 x 2 = 4; 4 + 4 = 8; 8 x 10 = 80;
b) 7 x 2 = 14; 14 x 2 = 28; 28 x 3 = 84)
Extension: 64 marbles (8 x 4 x 2 = 64)

4. **Light bar logic**: **a)** 18, 24; **b)** 81, 75
(Hint: 1 and 7 or 4 and 5 light bars)
Extension: **a)** 112, 113; **b)** 511, 311

5. **Decimal delight**: **a)** 4.27; **b)** 6.057
(Hint: 4.72 is bigger than 4.5)
Extension: 13.5, 13.57, 13.578, 13.58, 13.587

6. **Make that sum**: **a)** 12 x 3 – 4; **b)** 1 x 2 + 34
(Hint: You can put the numbers together.)
Extension: **a)** 12 – (3 x 4) or (1 + 2 – 3) x 4 or
12 ÷ 3 – 4 or 1 – 2 – 3 + 4
b) 12 ÷ 3 ÷ 4 or 1 x 2 + 3 – 4

7. **Cinema seats**: **a)** 28 tickets; **b)** 133 tickets
(Hint: **a)** There will be 26 tickets then BA then BB;
b) There will be 133 tickets then FA, FB and FC.)
Extension: **a)** MM; **b)** TY

8. **Cars and trucks**: **a)** 54 cars and 24 trucks;
b) 225 cars
(Hint: They are in groups of 13.)
Extension: 160 trucks

9. **What number am I?**: 76 145
(Hint: When you get an answer, check it against each clue to confirm that it is correct.)
Extension: Answers will vary.

10. **Equal notes**: 2 of each note
(Hint: 1 of each equals $185, 3 of each equals $555)
Extension: 4 x $5, 4 x $20, 4 x $50

11. **Multiplication mystery**: **a)** 7; **b)** 12
(Hint: **a)** 7 x 7 = 49; **b)** 12 x 12 = 144)
Extension: **a)** 8 (2 x 2 x 2 x 2 x 2 x 2 = 64);
b) 11 (The 61st odd number is 121.)

ISBN 978 1 4202 9396 8

Number and Algebra

Answers 2

12. **Third biggest**: **a)** 86 342; **b)** 55 344
(Hint: **a)** 86 432 then 86 423;
b) 55 443 then 55 434)
Extension: 97 534

13. **Postage paid**: $20
(Hint: $5 + (60 c x 25) = $20)
Extension: 62 letters and small packages altogether

14. **Seems too hard**: **a)** 50; **b)** 12
(Hint: It is the same as **a)** 2 x 25 and **b)** 1 x 12.)
Extension: **a)** 17 000; **b)** 12 600

15. **Decimal hunt**: Biggest 54.6; Smallest 54.2
(Hint: 54 ÷ 6 = 9; 54 ÷ 2 = 27)
Extension: Biggest 36.18; Smallest 22.11

16. **Radio waves**: **a)** 98.2; **b)** 99.1
(Hint: Half of 1.8 is 0.9.)
Extension: 104.7

17. **Biggest product**: **a)** 1284; **b)** 1312
(Hint: **a)** 321 x 4; **b)** 41 x 32)
Extension: **a)** 38 024 (5432 x 7) and 37 961 (5423 x 7); **b)** 39 566 (73 x 542) and 39 368 (74 x 532)

18. **Coin count**: **a)** 31 coins; **b)** $1.55
(Hint: **a)** 30 is the first number in the 2 times, 5 times and 6 times tables; **b)** 31 x 5 cents = $1.55, the smallest amount of money Katrina could have.)
Extension: **a)** 71 coins; **b)** $3.55

19. **Consecutive numbers**: **a)** 12, 13, 14; **b)** 22
(Hint: **a)** 39 ÷ 3 = 13, the middle number;
b) 72 ÷ 3 – 24; 22 + 24 + 26= 72)
Extension: 56 (48 + 52 + 56 = 156)

20. **Up and down**: 51 and 52
Extension: 14.5 and 13

21. **Quadley numbers**: 15, 26, 37, 51, 59, 62, 73, 95
(Hint: 48 and 84 are not quadleys, because they contain a 4.)
Extension: 159, 951

22. **Letters and numbers**: **a)** Y = 3 and Z = 8;
b) P = 8 and Q = 4
(Hint: **a)** 3 + 8 = 11 and 3 x 8 = 24;
b) 8 + 4 = 12 and 8 x 4 = 32)
Extension: 5 (The numbers are 4, 7 and 9)

ISBN 978 1 4202 9396 8

Number and Algebra

Answers 3

23. Phone numbers: **a)** 2 9999 3026;
b) 2 9900 0709
(Hint: Put the highest digits to the left in the biggest places.)
Extension: **a)** 2 9920 0000 and 2 9911 0000; **b)** 2 9900 0002 and 2 9900 0011

24. Number code: **a)** 27; **b)** 45
(Hint: 27 + 27 + 2 = 56)
Extension: 7 and 6

25. Notes: **a)** \$95; **b)** \$5 + \$10 + \$100 + \$20 + \$20 + \$20
(Hint: **a)** \$5 + \$10 +\$10 + \$20 + \$50 = \$95; **b)** \$5 + \$10 + \$100 + \$20 + \$20 + \$20 = \$175)
Extension: 3 (\$100 + \$100 + \$50 + \$50 + \$20 + \$20 + \$20 + \$10 + \$10 + \$10 + \$5 + \$5 = \$400)

26. Computer rules: **a)** 139; **b)** 220
(Hint: The rule is multiply the number by itself and then take away 5.)
Extension: Divide by 2 then add 4

27. Computer cruncher: Divide by 2 and then add the number as a decimal.
(Hint: Because the answer is smaller, it must either be dividing or subtracting.)
Extension: 21 (The rule is minus 1.5, then multiply by 2. Or, multiply by 2, then minus 3.)

28. Palindromic pals: **a)** 20; **b)** 884 488
(Hint: 1001, 1111, 1221 … 2772, 2882, 2992)
Extension: **a)** 23 232 (3462 + 2643 = 6105; 6105 + 5016 = 11 121; 11 121 + 12 111 = 23 232); **b)** Answers will vary.

29. Snakes and Ladders: 39
(Hint: 41 + 21 − 23 = 39)
Extension: 15 moves

30. Spilt milk: 8610
(Hint: It must end in 5 or 0 and be in the 3 times table.)
Extension: 8984

31. Short cut: **a)** 12; **b)** 30
(Hint: 81 x 6 – 79 x 6 is the same as 2 x 6.)
Extension: **a)** 707; **b)** 100

32. Pizza party: 28 slices
(Hint: 8 + 8 + 8 + 4)
Extension: $\frac{7}{8}$ pizza

ISBN 978 1 4202 9396 8

33. **Calculator challenge**: 25 ÷ 5 x 2
(Hint: The difference between multiplying and dividing by 5 is 25 times.)
Extension: **a)** 64; **b)** 125 (This is the same as multiplying by itself twice.)

34. **Christmas lights**: **a)** 24th place; **b)** 7 places
(Hint: 24 is in both the 6 times and 8 times tables.)
Extension: 120 seconds or 2 minutes

35. **James Frond**: **a)** PLEASE HELP!; **b)** ON THE WAY
(Hint: **a)** Each number is 1 before its letter place in the alphabet; **b)** Each number is 1 after its letter place in the alphabet.)
Extension: Answers will vary.

36. **Bookworm**: 32
(Hint: 14 + 15 + 16 = 45; 16 x 2 = 32)
Extension: **a)** 52 pages (1 + 2 + 51 + 52 = 106); **b)** 96 pages (1 + 2 + 95 + 96 = 194)

37. **Shoe sizes**: **a)** My sister's shoe size = $2\frac{1}{2}$, my shoe size = $4\frac{1}{2}$; **b)** My shoe size = $4\frac{1}{2}$, Mum's shoe size = 7 and Dad's shoe size = $9\frac{1}{2}$
(Hint: $2\frac{1}{2} + 4\frac{1}{2} = 7$, and the difference is 2)
Extension: $2\frac{1}{2}$ (The other sizes are 3, 4, and 6)

38. **Petals**: **a)** 29 petals left; **b)** 10th day
(Hint: 1, 3, 6, 10, 15, 21, 28, 36, 45, 50)
Extension: 17 days

39. **All values**: **a)** 5; **b)** 7
(Hint: **a)** \$1, \$2, \$2, \$5, \$10;
b) \$1, \$2, \$2, \$5, \$10, \$10, \$20, \$50)
Extension: 22 coins (1c, 2c, 2c, 19 x 5c)

40. **Buying letters**: **a)** \$3.10; **b)** \$2.80; **c)** \$2.50
(Hint: **a)** 4 x 50 cents + 4 x 20 cents + 3 x 10 cents; **b)** 4 x 50c + 3 x 20c + 2 x 10c;
c) 3 x 50c + 4 x 20c + 2 x 10c)
Extension: Answers will vary.

41. **Dogs and cats**: **a)** 3 more cat steps; **b)** 36 steps
(Hint: 1 dog step covers $1\frac{1}{2}$ cat steps.)
Extension: 80 m

42. **Who am I?**: 86 042
(Hint: 86 420, then 86 402, then 86 240, then 86 204)
Extension: 15 379

43. **Skip count**: 56 and 112
(Hint: 7 and 8 have no common factors.)
Extension: 210, 420, 630, 840

ISBN 978 1 4202 9396 8

Number and Algebra — Answers 5

44. Peter in a lift: Level 9
(Hint: 3 is $\frac{1}{3}$ of 9)
Extension: Level 8 (If he got on at level 2, he would now be on level 8.)

45. Busy pool: 16
(Hint: Lanes = 64, 32, 16, 8, 4, 2)
Extension: 10 people (21 + 3 – 10 = 14; 14 is $\frac{2}{3}$ of 21)

46. Computer virus: **a)** 12 seconds; **b)** 2.25 bytes
(Hint: **a)** 3, 6, 12, 24, 48, 96, 192, 384, 768, 1536; **b)** 0.75 + 1.5 = 2.25)
Extension: 364 bytes
(1 + 3 + 9 + 27 + 81 + 243 = 364)

47. Find the numbers: **a)** 1, 7, 11, 13, 17, 19, 23, 29, 31, 37; **b)** 61, 65, 67, 71, 73, 79
Extension: **a)** 1, 13, 17, 19, 23, 29, 31, 37, 41, 43, 47; **b)** 61, 67, 71, 73, 79, 83, 89, 97

48. Nectar search: **a)** 34th flower; **b)** 11 flowers
(Hint: The next flower the butterfly visits is the sum of the 2 previous flowers.)
Extension: 7th ring (Each ring has 4 times as many flowers as the previous ring.)

49. Digit find: **a)** 8002, 8011, 8020, 8101, 8110, 8200, 9001, 9010, 9100; **b)** 1029, 1038, 1047, 1056, 1065, 1074, 1083, 1092
Extension: **a)** 7003, 7030, 7300, 7012, 7021, 7111, 7120, 7102, 7210, 7201; **b)** 9000, 8100, 8010, 8001, 7200, 7110, 7101, 7020

50. Ages and ages: Mum is 31, I am 9.
(Hint: 279 is in the 9 times table.)
Extension: Dad is 35, my sister is 11
(86 – 31 – 9 = 46; 35 + 11 = 46; 35 – 11 = 24)

51. Arrows of change: **a)** 14; **b)** 360
(Hint: ↓ = divide by 5 and ← = – 2)
Extension: 7 (631 – 2 – 2 – 2 = 625; 625 ÷ 5 ÷ 5 ÷ 5 ÷ 5 = 1)

52. Franco's Fresh Fish: **a)** \$56; **b)** 26 fish
(Hint: 4 x \$5 + 6 x \$4 + 4 x \$3 = \$56)
Extension: 120 items (For every 1 paid item, you get 10 free items. 132 ÷ 11 = 12; 12 x 10 = 120)

53. Cricket gear: **a)** \$91; **b)** \$12; **c)** \$9
(Hint: The difference between the 2 total costs is 3 pairs of pads, which cost \$36.)
Extension: Sixteen 6s and four 1s

ISBN 978 1 4202 9396 8

54. Splat: 3 ways:
1: 1, 5, x 5
2: 2, 4, x 5
3: 3, x 2, x 5
Extension: 22 (Try to make each total until you reach one that cannot be made.)

55. Hoopla: **a)** 4 ways:
1: 3 + 3 + 3
2: 9 + 0 + 0
3: 7 + 1 + 1
4: 5 + 3 + 1
b) 3 ways:
1: 0 + 1 + 9
2: 0 + 3 + 7
3: 0 + 5 + 5
c) 12 ways:
1: 1 + 1 + 19
2: 1 + 3 + 17
3: 1 + 5 + 15
4: 1 + 7 + 13
5: 1 + 9 + 11
6: 3 + 3 + 15
7: 3 + 5 + 13
8: 3 + 7 + 11
9: 3 + 9 + 9
10: 5 + 5 + 11
11: 5 + 7 + 9
12: 7 + 7 + 7
Extension: 3 ways:
1: 13 + 19 + 19
2: 15 + 17 + 19
3: 17 + 17 + 17

56. Same number: **a)** 3.3; **b)** 3.6
(Hint: **a)** 20 – 10.1 = 9.9 and 9.9 ÷ 3 = 3.3; **b)** 39.4 – 25 = 14.4 and 14.4 ÷ 4 = 3.6)
Extension: **a)** 10; **b)** 6

57. Football jumpers: 6 possible numbers:
1: 4 and 16
2: 5 and 25
3: 6 and 36
4: 7 and 49
5: 8 and 64
6: 9 and 81
(Hint: It must be a 1-digit number and a 2-digit number to make a total 3-digit number.)
Extension: 14 goals and 7 behinds

58. Screen code: **a)** 2; **b)** 1, 7 and 0
(Hint: 1.On 2.Off 3.On 4.On 5.On 6.Off 7.On.)
Extension: **a)** 51; **b)** 991

ISBN 978 1 4202 9396 8

59. Soft toy pets: **a)** 6 ways:
1: Cat $10 + snail $1 + snail $1
2: Octopus $8 + bird $2 + bird $2
3: Ladybird $6 + starfish $5 + snail $1
4: Ladybird $6 + dog $4 + bird $2
5: Starfish $5 + starfish $5 + bird $2
6: Dog $4 + dog $4 + dog $4
b) 6 ways:
1: Caterpillar $16 + bird $2 + bird $2
2: Cat $10 + octopus $8 + bird $2
3: Cat $10 + ladybird $6 + dog $4
4: Cat $10 + starfish $5 + starfish $5
5: Octopus $8 + octopus $8 + dog $4
6: Octopus $8 + ladybird $6 + ladybird $6
Extension: Answers will vary.

60. Different numbers: **a)** 15; **b)** 17
(Hint: A = 24, B = 3)
Extension: 3 (Any number divided by itself equals 1, so the sum is 1 x 1 + 1 + 1 = 3)

61. Paint the fence: **a)** 2 days; **b)** 8 hours or 1 day
(Hint: 1 painter can paint 50 m in a day.)
Extension: 6 cans (1 can = 16 m, and with 2 coats Basil is painting 282 m of fence)

62. Healthy Tum: $3.60
(Hint: 2 sandwiches cost $7.20 and 1 coffee costs $2.40.)
Extension: $5.60 (Health bars cost 80 c each.)

63. Number search: 6348.3
(Hint: The 3s must be 3 places apart.)
Extension: Answers will vary.

64. Triple squares: 194, 419, 491, 914, 941
(1, 4 and 9 are the only 1-digit numbers that are made when a number is multiplied by itself.)
Extension: 235, 238, 253, 258, 283, 285, 325, 328, 352, 358, 382, 385, 523, 528, 532, 538, 582, 583, 823, 825, 832, 835, 852, 853

65. Make a sum: There are many answers that work. See how many you can find. For example,
a) 4 x 4 + 4 – 4; **b)** 4 + 4 – 4 – 4;
c) (4 ÷ 4) + (4 ÷ 4); **d)** 44 – (4 ÷ 4)
Extension: **a)** 444 ÷ 4 – 4; **b)** Answers will vary.

66. Lightning Lad: Point L
(Hint: Every 12th point, he will return to A.)
Extension: D (96 ÷ 12 = 8, plus 4 more points = 100)

ISBN 978 1 4202 9396 8

Number and Algebra

Answers 8

67. **Quarters and halves**: 8
(Hint: Beth counts 4 times as many numbers as Andrew, 32 numbers compared to 8.)
Extension: $13\frac{1}{4}$ and $13\frac{1}{2}$

68. **Postie Nat**: **a)** 21.6 km; **b)** 100.8 km
(Hint: **a)** $\frac{1}{4}$ of 28.8 is 7.2;
b) (7.2 x2) + (14.4 x 2) + (28.8 x 2) = 100.8)
Extension: 111 items (91 letters, 7 magazines, 11 parcels)

69. **Buying stamps**: **a)** 12 of each; **b)** 40 cents change; **c)** 30
(Hint: 60c + 50c + 5c = 80 c; 12 x 80 c = $9.60)
Extension: 700 g ($3.65 – $1.20 = $2.45; $2.45 ÷ 35 c = 7; 7 x 100 g = 700 g)

70. **Dog, cat and horse**: 600 g
(Hint: 8800 ÷ 44 = 200 g = 1 part)
Extension: 490 kg (The horse is 490 times heavier than the cat. 490 + 7 + 1 = 498)

71. **Grandfather clock**: **a)** 240; **b)** Saturday, 11 am, 6 days later
(Hint: Figure out how many times the clock will strike in one day.)
Extension: The clock will strike 228 times a day.

72. **Light it up**: **a)** 0, 4, 6, 7, 9, 11, 14, 17, 41, 71;
b) 28, 38, 58, 60, 66, 68, 69, 80, 82, 83, 85, 86, 88, 89, 90, 96, 98, 99
Extension: **a)** 100, 106, 108, 109, 128, 138, 158, 160, 166, 168, 169, 180, 182, 183, 185, 186, 188, 189, 190, 196, 198, 199, 200;
b) 9711

73. **Well batted**: 4 ways:

1: 6 + 3 + 1
2: 6 + 2 + 2
3: 4 + 4 + 2
4: 4 + 3 + 3

Extension: 5 ways:

1: 6 + 6 + 6 + 3 + 1
2: 6 + 6 + 6 + 2 + 2
3: 6 + 6 + 4 + 4 + 2
4: 6 + 6 + 4 + 3 + 3
5: 6 + 4 + 4 + 4 + 4

74. **Multiply**: **a)** 96; **b)** 20
(Hint: **a)** 5 x 4 x 3 x 2 x 1 = 120; 4 x 3 x 2 x 1 = 24; **b)** 3x 2 x 1 = 6)
Extension: **a)** 1 and 2 (1 has no numbers smaller than it and 2 x 1 = 2);
b) 6 (6 x 5 x 4 x 3 x 2 x 1 = 720)

ISBN 978 1 4202 9396 8

Number and Algebra — Answers 9

75. Round robin: **a)** Swifts 31 goals, Sharks and Scorpions 24 goals each; **b)** 16 goals
(Hint: Start with around 26 goals each.)
Extension: 28 matches (In a round robin, each team must play each other team once.)

76. Starting point: **a)** 102; **b)** 12
(Hint: **a)** 102 ÷ 2 = 51; 51 ÷ 3 = 17;
b) 12 – 10 = 2; 2 ÷ 2 = 1; 1 x 5 = 5)
Extension: 26

77. Plumber's bill: $560
(Hint: (7 x $60) + (1 x $50) + (1 x $40) + (2 x $25) = $560)
Extension: **a)** $1100 ($1210 ÷ 11 = $110; $1210 – $110 = $1100); **b)** $220
($1100 – $110 = $990; $1210 – $990 = $220)

78. By itself: 7
(Hint: 7 x 7 = 49 and 7 x 10 – 21 = 49)
Extension: 4 (4 x 4 x 4 = 64 and
4 x 10 + 4 + 4 + 4 + 4 + 4 + 4 = 64)

79. Exchange rate: **a)** $200; **b)** $50
(Hint: 12 000 ÷ 60 = 200 and 12 000 ÷ 80 = 150)
Extension: $40.50 (3600 ÷ 80 = 45;
45 ÷ 10 = 4.5; 45 – 4.5 = $40.50)

80. Maximum and minimum: **a)** Eastville changed by 16.6 degrees; **b)** Eastville = 13 degrees, Westville = 24.3 degrees, Northville = 28.3 degrees
(Hint: Westville 14.4 degrees, Northville 9.8 degrees)
Extension: 21.5 degrees (21.3 + 31.5 + 33.2 = 86;
86 ÷ 4 = 21.5)

81. Cheeky rabbit: 16 five-hop moves
(Hint: Highest point: 5, 8, 11, 14, 17, 20, 23, 26, 29, 32, 35, 38, 41, 44, 47, 50)
Extension: 72 days (Each day it has 7 less hairs.)

82. Find my number: 3747.1
(Hint: The two 7s must be 2 places apart.)
Extension: 9 (7743.1 – 7734.1)

ISBN 978 1 4202 9396 8

83. Descendigital numbers: 5 numbers: 4321, 4320, 4310, 4210, 3210
Extension: **a)** 10 numbers: 5432, 5431, 5430, 5421, 5420, 5410, 5321, 5320, 5310, 5210; **b)** 15 numbers: 63 210, 64 210, 64 310, 64 320, 64 321, 65 210, 65 310, 65 320, 65 321, 65 410, 65 420, 65 421, 65 430, 65 431, 65 432

84. Symbol shifter: **a)** 19; **b)** 172; **c)** 82
(Hint: [#] means multiply by 3 and take away 2)
Extension: **a)** 35; **b)** 290 ([^] means to multiply the number by itself twice and then add 2.)

85. Generous Gran: **a)** $240; **b)** Grandson $\frac{1}{2}$, son $\frac{1}{4}$, cousin $\frac{1}{12}$, niece $\frac{1}{24}$
(Hint: Grandson $120, son $60, cousin $20, niece $10)
Extension: 10 people (Divide by 2 each time)

86. Number line: B, D, C, E, A
(Hint: Change all the fractions to twelfths.)
Extension: **a)** I, G, J, F, H; **b)** $2\frac{3}{10}$

87. Circular letter pattern: **a)** T; **b)** N
(Hint: It is the 46th letter in the pattern and 46 – 26 = 20, or T.)
Extension: R (The number value of the letter is doubling each time. A = 1, B = 2, D = 4, H = 8 . . . R is the 512th letter in the circular pattern.)

88. No more sevens: **a)** 64; **b)** 105, 107, 112
(Hint: 14, 21, 28, 35, 42, 49, 56 and 63 are all multiples of 7)
Extension: 55 (All even numbers and all numbers in the 20s and 120s will disappear.)

89. Pile Up: **a)** 10th move; **b)** 50
(Hint: **a)** 4, 3 then 7, 5 then 9, 6 then 10, 9 then 13, 11 then 15, 12, then 16, 15 then 19, 17, then 21, 18; **b)** 1, 2, 8, 14, 20, 26, 32, 38, 44, 50)
Extension: 3 times (Use a picture to help you find the answer.)

90. Phone book: **a)** 5250 names; **b)** 450 000 people
(Hint: **a)** 5 x 100 x 10.5;
b) 300 x 5 x 100 x 3 = 450 000)
Extension: 44 columns (10 + 7 + 4 + 3 = 24; 264 ÷ 24 = 11; 4 x 11 = 44)

91. Read all about it: **a)** 20 pages; **b)** $\frac{1}{12}$
(Hint: 120 – 48 – 40 – 12 = 20)
Extension: 64 pages (16 x 4 = 64)

ISBN 978 1 4202 9396 8

92. Harry's birthday: 57
(Hint: He is too old to be 24.)
Extension: 11 (The others are 3, 3 and 2 years old)

93. Blurred image: 804, 816, 828, 840, 852, 864, 876, 888, 900
(Hint: These numbers are multiples of 3 and 4.)
Extension: 1788 – First Fleet arrives in Australia

94. Different digits: A = 2, B = 5, C = 7
(Hint: This sum will only work if B = 5.)
Extension: D = 7, E = 2 or D = 1, E = 8

95. Rosie's cards: **a)** 12 answers: 236, 276, 326, 362, 372, 376, 632, 672, 726, 732, 736, 762; **b)** 12 answers: 2376, 2736, 3276, 3726, 3672, 3762, 6372, 6732, 7236, 7326, 7362, 7632
Extension: **a)** 14 answers: 213, 215, 231, 235, 241, 243, 245, 251, 253, 315, 321, 325, 341, 345; **b)** 20 answers: 3512, 3514, 4132, 4152, 4312, 4352, 4512, 4532, 5124, 5132, 5134, 5142, 5214, 5234, 5312, 5314, 5324, 5342, 5412, 5432

96. Letterboxes: **a)** 39; **b)** 68 and 72
(Hint: **a)** 37 + 39 + 41 = 117;
b) 68 + 70 + 72 = 210)
Extension: 26 houses (Add up all the even numbers until you reach 72.)

97. Landopoly: **a)** $3125 **b)** 1 house, 2 apartments and 3 blocks of land
(Hint: **a)** 5 x 5 x 5 x 5 x 5;
b) (1 x 625) + (2 x 125) + (3 x 5) = $890)
Extension: $12 500 (5 x 10 x 5 x 10 x 5 = $12 500)

98. Divider's delight: 64
(Hint: 32, 16, 8, 4, 2, 1)
Extension: 112 (56, 28, 14, 7)

99. Lighthouses: **a)** Once every 300 seconds (5 minutes); **b)** 7 times
(Hint: **a)** 300 is the first number in the 20 times, 25 times and 30 times tables; **b)** At 60, 100, 120, 150, 180, 200 and 240 seconds)
Extension: Once every 11 seconds (3 x 5 = 15; 165 ÷ 15 = 11)

100. Chess pieces: **a)** 24 pieces; **b)** $\frac{3}{32}$
(Hint: **a)** 8 is $\frac{1}{8}$ of 64; **b)** $\frac{6}{64} = \frac{3}{32}$)
Extension: 31 matches (16 + 8 + 4 + 2 + 1)

ISBN 978 1 4202 9396 8

Measurement and Geometry Answers 12

1. **Baby elephants**: **a)** Zazu weighs 405 kg and Bazeri weighs 595 kg; **b)** 12 years old
(Hint: If they differ by 190 kg, they must both be 95 kg away from 500 kg.)
Extension: 815 kg, 830 kg, 845 kg
(3290 kg – 800 kg = 2490 kg;
2490 kg ÷ 3 = 830 kg. 815 is halfway between 800 and 830, so they must all differ by 15 kg.)

2. **Distances**: **a)** 0.8 km; **b)** 0.65 m
(Hint: **a)** 0.8 is halfway between 0.6 and 1.0; **b)** 0.65 is halfway between 0.3 and 1.0.)
Extension: $\frac{255}{256}$ (Multiply 64 by 4, as the arrow is a quarter of a metre from the bullseye.)

3. **Flight to Portsville**: 875 km per hour
(Hint: 2625 ÷ 3 = 875)
Extension: 1:35 pm (The flight takes 4 hours and 10 minutes if the flight is 40 minutes late, then take away 2 hours for the time difference.)

4. **Scale trail**: **a)** About 13 cm; **b)** 4 mm
(Hint: **a)** 325 ÷ 25 = 13; **b)** 1 mm shows 2.5 km on the map.)
Extension: 1 cm = 325 km

5. **Vegie patch**: **a)** 36 square m; **b)** 35 square m
(Hint: **a)** 6 m x 6 m square; **b)** 7 m x 5 m rectangle)
Extension: **a)** 100 square m (80 pieces that are 50 cm long is the same as 40 pieces that are 1 m long.); **b)** 4 square m (40 pieces of 20 cm long is the same as 8 pieces that are 1 m long.)

6. **Right-angled clock**: 10 times
(Hint: There will be a right angle twice every hour, whenever the hands are apart exactly 3 of the 12 units on the clock face, e.g. 3:00 and about 3:33.)
Extension: About 12:32, 1:05, 1:38, 2:11, 2:43, 3:17, 3:49, 4:22, 4:55, 5:25

ISBN 978 1 4202 9396 8

Measurement and Geometry

Answers 13

7. **Bozo turns**: **a)** Between the snack bar and the trapeze; **b)** $3\frac{5}{8}$ turns
(Hint: Think of each of the things as points on a compass.)
Extension: 8 turns (Each time you turn $\frac{1}{8}$ turn further than the previous turn.)

8. **Curious ant**: **a)** 9 edges; **b)** 49.5 cm
(Hint: Complete the 4 base edges first.)
Extension: 15.5 cm

9. **All the squares**: 30 squares
(Hint: Sixteen 1 x 1 squares, nine 2 x 2 squares, four 3 x 3 squares, one 4 x 4 square)
Extension: 55 squares

10. **Washing day**: **a)** 42.5 L; **b)** 100 L
(Hint: As the machine loses 5 L, it fills with 2.5 L.)
Extension: 2.35 kg (4.7 kg – 1.5 kg – 0.85 kg = 2.35 kg)

11. **Where in line?**: Frank, David, Gita, Eric, Ben, Anna, Harry, Carlos
(Hint: To be to the right or left of someone you do not need to be right next to them.)
Extension: Answers will vary.

12. **Horizontal and vertical**: **a)** 27, 37, 57;
b) 14, 17, 41, 71
Extension: **a)** 511; **b)** 1113

13. **Travel times**: **a)** 110.1 m; **b)** 6606 m
(Hint: Divide each by 10.)
Extension: 60 km

14. **Twelve hours**: **a)** 270 minutes; **b)** 660 minutes
(Hint: There would need to be 120 minutes in every hour.)
Extension: **a)** 9:26 am; **b)** 5:10 pm

15. **Divided rectangle**: **a)** 8 right angles;
b) 18 smaller angles
(Hint: Look at the centre top, bottom left and right.)
Extension: **a)** 14 triangles; **b)** Rhombus;
c) 14 triangles

16. **Hollow cube**: 64 faces
Extension: Edges = 24, vertices (corners) = 16

17. **Three vehicles**: 41
(Hint: 41 x 24 g = 984 g)
Extension: 14 vehicles

ISBN 978 1 4202 9396 8

18. Paper folding: 32 right angles
(Hint: 8 rectangles x 4)
Extension: 14 right angles

19. Split hexagon: **a)** Any 2 adjoining sections, such as 1 and 2, 2 and 3, and so on;
b) Any 3 adjoining sections, such as 1, 2 and 3;
c) Each individual section is an equilateral triangle.
(Hint: Try colouring in the sections to see the individual shapes.)
Extension: **a)** 8 right angles; **b)** 20 angles less than a right angle

20. Rainy days: January to June 875 mm, July to December 125 mm
(Hint: Divide 1000 by 8.)
Extension: **a)** 84 mm; **b)** September 54 mm, October 18 mm, November 6 mm

21. Full of water: **a)** 200 mL; **b)** 8 kg
(Hint: 10 x 5 x 4 = 200)
Extension: 16 hours and 40 minutes

22. Packing boxes: 16
(Hint: 4 will fit side by side widthwise and 4 will fit on top of each other.)
Extension: 42 boxes (7 x 2 x 3 = 42)

23. Alphabetical move: 3 moves: MPBT, MBPT, BMPT
Extension: 4 moves: WCJR, CWJR, CJWR, CJRW

24. Fractional time: **a)** $\frac{1}{520}$; **b)** $\frac{1}{66}$
(Hint: **a)** There are 52 weeks in a year and 10 years in a decade; **b)** 12 + 12 + 12 + 12 + 12 + 6)
Extension: **a)** $\frac{1}{52}$; **b)** $\frac{1}{200}$

25. Squares from squares: 9, 16, 25
(Hint: These are 3 x 3, 4 x 4 and 5 x 5.)
Extension: 27, 64 and 125 cubes (These are 3 x 3 x 3, 4 x 4 x 4 and 5 x 5 x 5)

ISBN 978 1 4202 9396 8

Answers 15

1. **Spinning wheel**: **a)** $\frac{1}{6}$; **b)** $\frac{1}{8}$
   (Hint: 3 tickets still left out of 18)
   Extension: 11
2. **Different colours**: **a)** $\frac{1}{3}$; **b)** $\frac{3}{8}$; **c)** $\frac{3}{7}$
   (Hint: The chances increase as the shells decrease in number.)
   Extension: 14
3. **Basketball blitz**: **a)** 39 goals; **b)** 17 goals
   (Hint: **a)** 10 x 6 = 60; 60 – 4 – 12 – 5 = 39; **b)** To average 11 goals per game, Miranda must have a total of 77 goals for all 7 games.)
   Extension: 3 (9.75 x 4 = 39. Hannah must have scored three 10s and one 9 to have an average of 9.75 out of 10.)
4. **Hair and shoes**: **a)** The fraction of students whose shoe colours and hair colours either were the same or different; **b)** The fraction of students who were in the survey.
   Extension: **a)** 23 students; **b)** 23 students (4 students in the class did not take part in the survey, so we don't know their answers.)
5. **Dice roll**: **a)** 36; **b)** $\frac{1}{6}$; **c)** $\frac{1}{6}$; **d)** $\frac{1}{3}$
   Extension: **a)** $\frac{5}{12}$; **b)** $\frac{4}{9}$
6. **Trainspotting champions**: 45
   (Hint: 30 + 15)
   Extension: $\frac{9}{110}$ (After 6 people from Flynn win an award of excellence, there are 9 left out of a total 110 who could win the Choo Choo Cup.)
7. **Digit chance**: $\frac{1}{3}$
   (Hint: $\frac{1}{3}$ of the digits are even.)
   Extension: $\frac{1}{3}$
8. **Days of chance**: $\frac{31}{365}$ or $\frac{31}{366}$
   (Hint: It could be a leap year.)
   Extension: **a)** $\frac{91}{365}$ or $\frac{91}{366}$;
   b) $\frac{1}{365}$ or $\frac{1}{366}$
9. **Average performance**: 22
   (Hint: 40 – 5 – 11 = 24. 22, 1, 1)
   Extension: 26
10. **Decks of cards**: $\frac{1}{26}$
    (Hint: 104 cards. 2 are aces of spades and 2 are aces of clubs. $\frac{4}{104} = \frac{2}{52} = \frac{1}{26}$)
    Extension: **a)** $\frac{7}{100}$; **b)** $\frac{39}{100}$; **c)** $\frac{20}{100}$ or $\frac{1}{5}$

ISBN 978 1 4202 9396 8